Logic Lists English: Meaningful Words Volume Three

By
Tony Sandy

DragonEye Publishing

Logic List English: Meaningful Words - Volume 3
Copyright © 2018 By Tony Sandy

All rights reserved. No part of this book may be reproduced, by any means or in any form whatsoever without written permission from the author and Publisher, except for brief quotation embodied in literary articles or reviews.

Publisher info. Contact
DragonEye Publishing
753A Linden Pl.
Elmira, New York, 14901

For Questions Phone: 1-(607)-333-5256

For information about our books, and for special discounts for single / bulk purchases, please contact DragonEye Publishing Ordering Dept. at:
Website: DragonEyePublishers.com
Email: Orders@DragonEyePublishers.com

To request one of our authors for speaking engagements or book signings, please contact DragonEye Publishing Publicity Dept. at: Directors@DragonEyePublishers.com

Published by
, an Imprint of DragonEye Publishing

ISBN 13: 978-1-61500-205-4 (Paperback)
ISBN 13: 978-1-61500-210-8 (EBook)

Library of Congress Control Number: 2018938499

DragonEye Publishing, First Edition: 2018
First Printing: April 10, 2018

10 9 8 7 6 5 4 3 2 1

Manufactured in the United States of America

INTRODUCTION TO MAIN SECTION

This volume is about meaning. It must be remembered that words are just abstract sounds or written symbols, until they associated in your mind with reality. Through this linking, understanding comes.

Comprehension, like physical skill, flows through usage. This is how I sorted the material for the books in the first place. If a column snagged at a certain place or places, I knew it needed alteration or further alteration to the forms being used (even now I know that the material could be further refined - not just individual columns but some sections could be broken down still further into subsections, in some cases).

The material is arranged by root form and single sequences of meaning, rather than confusing variations of form and multiple definitions. If you have to think about the definition of a word, then the sequence is interrupted instead of flowing, which is useless to the learner. Real, obvious connections jump instantly into the mind, whereas contrived ones don't- instead having to be consciously memorised, a word form at a time. For instance, the word chain from the same route, meaning to 'break' (rupture, erupt, disrupt, abrupt but then corrupt, which has no obvious connection except in spelling). This is only of use to the highly skilled, not the novice. It is all these twists and turns that cause confusion to the learner, especially in areas of spelling and meaning. My pattern teaching method, hopefully will help overcome some of these difficulties.

Alternative meanings for various forms of a word, can be so strong that they throw out the definition sequence in the mind – for instance collective means altogether but the alternative definition of communist farming method, can be so strong that it drowns out the lesser used meaning.

Reading is easier than writing because you don't have to understand word order, tense, punctuation, spelling, verb forms or anything else to do with grammar. All you have to do is decipher what the words are trying to tell you, at least roughly. Writing, which requires some rudimentary knowledge of grammar, means that to be understood, your handwriting has to be clear enough to be readable as well as grammatically sound enough, to make sense to the reader or it fails to convey a meaningful message to them (you know from your own reactions when you've got it and need to look out for it in others, to see if they understand what you mean). Crosswords are a good way of checking your understanding of the meaning of a word from the clues given but not the more complex ones as they rely on knowledge in more depth (not necessarily the answers themselves but the clues given). This is appropriate only to the highly skilled in the language / culture, not the novice starting out in it.

Common abbreviations have been used in some of these lists, in order to conserve space for other items in the list. Note how the meaning of a word combination can change depending on whether one of the duo is in front or behind the other. Some foreign learners retain not only their original accent but syntax and grammar as well, including word order differences as well as added or removed words, appropriate to their original tongue but not the new language. Tenses too can be affected, where there is discrepancies between the two languages.

If you can replace one word with another, without changing the meaning, then you know both terms are equal (synonyms). I have collected such words together as well as common but opposite forms (antonyms). Also here you will find related terms and definitions than confuse because of their divergent meaning from the original. Notice how synonyms can appear in different phrases, depending upon the most fashionable form at a particular time in the past (e.g. insane, crazy, mad, having a screw loose etc).

Please note that a lot of these word groups are jargon or slang, belonging to a particular group of people, region, trade or profession.

INTRODUCTION TO REAL WORLD SUBSECTION

The second part of this book is composed of real world items, subjective and objective terminology but mostly the latter. It is a journey of perception from the depths of space into this world, through natural and human landscapes, down to the smallest forms of life and existence on this planet. It also includes hierarchies, scales and classes, animal families and parts of wholes – that is contained environments, including bodies, engines, buildings, towns etc. (Usborne Books in The UK, produce similar, illustrated material to these ideas gathered here).

Meaningful terms have a real order that takes us down from the largest things in creation (universe, galaxy, solar system) to the smallest (atoms, molecules, bacteria). We take things apart to understand them and put them back together, to make them work. This includes the physical world (science) as well as our own minds (psychology and the soft sciences).

Meaning starts out in the far universe but comes right down to you, up close and personal (the culture of where you live, the people you know, the thoughts in your head about reality). Visiting another country – it's looks, smells, tastes, the habits of the indigenous population, are all things you have to get used to and that includes the language code. All you will hear at first is meaningless gobbledegook, rapidly spoken by those proficient in the language (which obviously isn't you). Then you will start to pick the odd sounds, the repeated phrase – learning the language bit by bit (adapting to the culture is easier, comparatively speaking). This is how we learn foreigners languages and they learn ours – in fact it is how we learned our own native tongue as we grew up (total immersion in the culture as with The Berlitz method). By the way, language and culture are inextricably mixed as one is born from the other.

See how you start out with generalised terms for subjects and work down to specifics, the item becoming the heading (coats, ties, shirts, hats as clothing in general, which can then become trilby, cap, boater etc). This can lead down even to proper names as in the company that produced the product, including the model (Ford Anglia, Cortina, Fusion etc). Proper names creep in as you become more specific and less generalised in subject matter (cars, football teams, fashion houses etc).

Another writer of this section might include words that are particular to their time and place (more local to their country, area, age group etc. including dialect – thee and thou for me and you, aye and nay for yes and no, book, burn, beck or gill for stream, loch, Lynn or mere for lake. You will also get nicknames like Chalky for someone with the surname of White, Taff for a Welshman, Mac for a Scotsman, Tommy for an Englishman etc.

Pictures, even in sequence, are simpler to understand than words because you can use different terms (but not illustrations) to try to explain or describe things and it may not immediately be apparent what the sense of the sentence is – whereas visual material is usually instantly clear, if recognizable.

As with the previous volumes, new words can be added to the columns or swapped for new ones. Even new columns can be created, based upon missed subject matter (some groups have been deliberately because the words involved were already covered in previous volumes or will be included in later ones).

The material gathered here is arbitrary. By that I mean the individual words could have been grouped together in new columns, bearing fresh headings. Thesaurus material as in Volume 3B, is like all material here – a mixture of analytical and associational ideas, clubbed together in what is hopefully useful forms.

CONTENTS

9   Words Related by Spelling & Meaning
55   The Real World
       The Physical World
73   Proper Nouns

SECTION ONE:- WORDS RELATED BY SPELLING AND MEANING

Logic List English: Meaningful Words - Volume 3

Legal	Sentient	Judge	Affect	Out
Legally	Sentience	Judicial	Effect	Outer
Legalize	Sentinel	Judiciary	Effective	Outermost
Legalization	Sense	Jurisdiction	Effectively	Outwards
Legislate	Sensor	Jurisprudence	Effectual	Outwardly
Legislation	Sensory	Jury	Efficacious	Outside
Legislator	Sensation	Jurist	Efficacy	Outing
Legislature	Sensitive	Justice	Ineffectual	In
Legitimate	Sensitivity	Justify	Ineffective	Inner
Legitimately	Sensitize	Injustice	Efficient	Inwards
Legitimize	Desensitize	Judicious	Efficiently	Inwardly
Legitimacy	Insensitive	Injudicious	Efficiency	Inside
Litigant	Insentivity	Misjudge	Inefficient	Innermost
Litigation	Insensate	Prejudice	.	.
Illicit	Insensible	Prejudicial	.	.
Illegal	.	.	.	.
Illegality	.	.	.	.
Illegitimate	.	.	.	.
Land	Joy	Electric	Term	Able
Inland	Joyful	Electrics	Terminus	Ability
Overland	Jovial	Electricity	Terminal	Ably
Landward	Jubilant	Electrical	Terminate	Capable
Landfall	Jubilation	Electrician	Termination	Capability
Landing	Jocund	Electrocute	Eliminate	Capacity
Landlubber	Jocular	Electrocution	Elimination	Enable
Landscape	Jocose	Electrify	Exterminate	Unable
Wetland	Enjoy	Electrification	Extermination	Incapable
Landlocked	Enjoyment	Electronic	Interminable	Incapacitated
Landslide	Overjoyed	Electrode	Interminably	Disable
Landed	Rejoice	Electrolysis	.	Disability
Landless	.	.	.	.
Landlord	.	.	.	.
Landlady	.	.	.	.

Equal	Ideal	Introduce	Continue	Number
Equally	Ideally	Introduction	Continual	Numeral
Equality	Idyll	Produce	Continually	Numerical
Equalize	Idyllic	Producer	Continuation	Numerate
Equalization	Idealize	Product	Continuance	Numeration
Equivalent	Idealization	Production	Continuous	Numeracy
Equivalence	Idealism	Productive	Continuously	Innumerate
Equate	Idealist	Productivity	Continuum	Numberless
Unequal	Idealistic	Reproduce	Continuity	Unnumbered
Inequality	Ideology	Reproduction	Discontinue	Innumerable
Equation	Ideologist	Reproductive	Discontinuous	Numerous
Equator	Ideological	Unproductive	Discontinuity	.
Announce	Value	Possible	Direct	Divide
Announcer	Valuable	Possibly	Directly	Divisor
Announcement	Valluables	Possibility	Directness	Divisible
Enunciate	Valuation	Impossible	Direction	Divisive
Enunciation	Valuer	Impossibility	Directional	Undivided
Pronounce	Evaluate	Potential	Indirect	Division
Pronounceable	Evaluation	Potentially	Directive	Divisional
Pronunciate	Invaluable	Potentiality	Director	Individual
Pronunciation	Devalue	Probable	Directorship	Individually
Denounce	Devaluation	Probability	Directorate	Individuality
Denounciation	Valueless	Improbable	Directorial	Individualism
Inform	Real	Psychiatry	Society	Nature
Information	Really	Psychiatrist	Social	Naturalist
Informative	Reality	Psychiatric	Socially	Natural
Informant	Realism	Psychology	Socialize	Naturally
Informer	Realistic	Psychologist	Socialization	Naturalistic
Misinform	Realistically	Psychological	Anti-social	Unnatural
Misinformation	Realist	Psychotherapy	Socialist	Supernatural
Disinformation	Unreal	Psychotherapy	Socialism	Naturist
Informal	Unrealistic	Psychoanalyse	Sociology	Naturism
Informally	Realize	Psychoanalyst	Sociologist	Naturalize
Informality	Realization	Psychonalysis	Sociological	.

Nation	New	Migrate	Emit	Hand
National	Newly	Migration	Emission	Unhand
Nationally	Newness	Migratory	Mission	Mishandle
Nationalist	Anew	Migrant	Missionary	Handicap
Nationalism	Renew	Immigrant	Emissary	Handler
Nationalize	Renewal	Immigration	Admit	Handle
Nationality	Renewable	Emigrate	Admitted	Underhand
International	Renovate	Emigration	Admission	Handy
Internationally	Renovation	Emigrant	Admittance	Handily
Multinational	News	Emigre	Admittedly	Handiness
Harmony	Memory	Pure	Incise	Length
Harmonize	Memorable	Purley	Incisive	Lengthy
Harmonious	Memorize	Purity	Incision	Lengthily
Harmoniously	Remember	Purist	Incisor	Lengthen
Disharmony	Memorial	Purification	Precise	Lengthways
Disharmonious	Commemorate	Puritan	Precisely	Lengthwise
Harmonic	Commemoration	Puritanism	Precision	Elongate
Harmonics	Memento	Puritanical	Concise	Along
Harmonica	Memoir	Impure	Concisely	Longer
Harmonium	Memorandum	Impurity	Conciseness	Longest
Local	Absent	Amateur	Bright	Modest
Locally	Absence	Amateurish	Brightly	Modestly
Locality	Absentee	Profession	Brighten	Modesty
Localize	Absenteeism	Professional	Brightness	Immodest
Locate	Absently	Professionally	Brilliant	Immodesty
Location	Presence	Professionalism	Brilliance	Moderate
Relocate	Present	Proficient	Dim	Moderately
Relocation	Presently	Proficiency	Dimly	Moderation
Dislocate	Presenter	Profess	Dimness	Moderator
Dislocation	Presentation	Professorship	Dimmer	Immoderate
Please	Ease	Name	Need	Negate
Pleasing	Easy	Nickname	Needs	Negation
Pleasant	Easily	Surname	Needful	Negative
Pleasantly	Easiness	Nameless	Needy	Abnegate
Pleasure	Unease	Unnamed	Necessity	Abnegation
Pleasurable	Uneasy	Nominal	Necessitate	Negligence
Unpleasant	Uneasily	Denominate	Necessary	Negligent
Displease	Uneasiness	Enumerate	Necessarily	Negligible
Displeasure	Disease	Enumeration	Unnecessary	Negligee
.	.	.	.	.
.	.	.	.	.
.	.	.	.	.
.	.	.	.	.

Logic List English: Meaningful Words - Volume 3

Note	Optimum	Circle	Force	Include
Notable	Optimal	Circular	Forcible	Inclusion
Notably	Optimize	Circuit	Forcibly	Inclusive
Notify	Optimism	Circuitry	Forceful	Preclude
Notification	Optimist	Encircle	Enforce	Exclude
Notifiable	Optimistic	Encirclement	Enforcement	Exclusion
Notice	Pessimism	Curculate	Enforceable	Exclusive
Noticeable	Pessimist	Circulation	Reinforce	Exclusiveness
Unnoticed	Pessimistic	Circuitous	Reinforcements	Exclusivity
Exist	Grade	Grateful	Image	Mass
Existent	Gradation	Gratefully	Imagery	Matter
Existence	Gradient	Gratefulness	Imagine	Material
Extant	Gradual	Gratitude	Imagination	Materialize
Coexist	Gradually	Ungrateful	Imaginary	Materialization
Coexistence	Ungraded	Ingratitude	Imaginable	Dematerialize
Existential	Graduate	Gratify	Imaginative	Materialism
Existentialism	Graduation	Gratifying	Unimaginative	Materialist
Existentialist	Postgraduate	Gratification	Unimaginable	Materialistic
Literate	Passion	Concept	Credit	Crime
Literacy	Passionate	Conception	Credible	Criminal
Literary	Impassioned	Conceptual	Credibility	Criminally
Literature	Compassion	Conceptualize	Credence	Criminality
Illiterate	Compassionate	Conceive	Discredit	Criminology
Illiteracy	Placid	Conceivable	Incredible	Criminologist
Legible	Passive	Conceivably	Credulous	Incriminate
Illegible	Impassive	Inconceivable	Incredulous	Incriminating
Illegibility	Impassivity	Misconception	Incredulity	Incrimination
Quiz	Intellect	Intent	Benefit	False
Quizzical	Intellectual	Intently	Beneficial	Falsely
Inquisition	Intelligent	Intense	Benevolent	Falseness
Inquisitor	Intelligently	Intensely	Benevolence	Falsity
Inquisitorial	Intelligence	Intensive	Benficence	Falsify
Inquisitive	Intelligible	Intensively	Beneficent	Falsification
Enquire	Intelligibility	Intensity	Benefaction	Fallacious
Enquiry	Intelligentsia	Intensify	Benefactor	Fallacy
Enquirer	Unintelligible	Intensification	Beneficiary	Falsehood
.	.	.	.	.
.	.	.	.	.
.	.	.	.	.
.	.	.	.	.
.	.	.	.	.

Final	Mystery	Regular	Repulse	Express
Finalist	Mysterious	Regularity	Repulsive	Expression
Finally	Mysteriously	Irregular	Repulsion	Expressive
Finale	Mystify	Irregularity	Revulsion	Repress
Finish	Mystification	Regulate	Repugnance	Repression
Finalize	Mystique	Regulation	Repugnant	Repressive
Finality	Mystic	Regulator	Attract	Suppress
Semifinal	Mystical	Deregulate	Attractive	Supression
Semifinalist	Mysticism	Deregulation	Attraction	Supressive
Technical	Defend	Possess	Sate	Pretence
Technically	Defender	Possession	Satiate	Pretend
Technician	Defence	Possessor	Satisfy	Pretender
Technology	Defensive	Disposses	Satisfying	Pretension
Technological	Defensively	Dispossession	Satisfactory	Pretentious
Technologist	Defensible	Repossess	Satisfaction	Unpretentious
Technocracy	Undefended	Repossession	Disatisfied	Genuine
Technocrat	Indefensible	Possessive	Disatisfaction	Genuinely
Technique	Defendant	Possessiveness	Unsatisfying	Genuiness
Capture	Concept	Vary	Voice	Nerve
Captor	Conception	Variable	Vocal	Nervy
Captive	Conceptual	Variant	Vocalize	Nervous
Captivity	Conceptualize	Variation	Vociferous	Nervously
Recapture	Conceive	Various	Vocalist	Nervousness
Capitulate	Conceivable	Invariable	Invoke	Neurotic
Capitulation	Conceivably	Variety	Invocation	Neurosis
Recapitulate	Inconceivable	Variegated	Vocabulary	Unnerved
Recapitulation	Preconceive	.	.	.
Obey	Observe	Motion	Close	Live
Obedient	Observer	Motionless	Closure	Alive
Obediently	Observable	Emotion	Disclose	Living
Obedience	Observatory	Emotional	Disclosure	Lively
Obeisance	Observation	Emotive	Enclose	Liveliness
Disobey	Unobserved	Motive	Enclosure	Enliven
Disobedient	Observant	Motivate	Foreclose	Livestock
Disobedience	Unobservant	Motivation	Foreclosure	Livelihood
.	.	.	.	.
.	.	.	.	.
.	.	.	.	.
.	.	.	.	.
.	.	.	.	.
.	.	.	.	.

Assemble	Trust	Patriot	Gene	Gravity
Assembly	Trusting	Patriotic	Genetic	Gravitate
Assemblage	Trustful	Patriotism	Genetics	Gravitation
Reassemble	Trusty	Unpatriotic	Geneticist	Gravitational
Ensemble	Trustworthy	Compatriot	Geneology	Levitate
Semblance	Entrust	Expatriate	Congenital	Levitation
Resemble	Distrust	Repariate	Genocide	Gravid
Resemblance	Distrustful	Repatriation	Genus	Levity
Humane	Mortal	Pass	Moral	Rational
Humanly	Mortality	Passing	Morally	Rationally
Humanitarian	Mortally	Passable	Morality	Rationality
Inhuman	Morgue	Passage	Moralize	Rationalize
Inhumane	Mortuary	Impasse	Amoral	Rationalism
Inhumanity	Immortal	Impassable	Immoral	Rationlist
Dehumanize	Immortality	Passport	Immorality	Rationale
Humanize	Immortalize	Passenger	Morale	Irrational
Revere	Convenient	Consider	Dependent	Digest
Reverence	Conveniently	Considering	Dependence	Digestion
Reverent	Convenience	Consideration	Dependency	Digestive
Reverently	Inconvenient	Considerate	Independent	Digestible
Reverential	Inconvenience	Considerately	Independently	Indigestible
Reverend	Incommode	Inconsiderate	Independence	Indigestion
Irreverent	Commodius	Considerable	Dependable	Ingest
Irreverence	Incommodiuos	Considerably	Dependability	Ingestion
Doubt	Invent	Sensuous	Insist	Tone
Doubter	Invention	Sensual	Insistent	Tonal
Doubtful	Inventor	Sensuality	Insistence	Tonality
Dubious	Inventive	Sensualist	Persist	Toneless
Doubtless	Inventiveness	Sensualism	Persistent	Toneless
Undoubted	Innovate	Sensational	Persistence	Atonal
Undoubtedly	Innovation	Sensationalism	Persevere	Intone
Indubitable	Innovator	Sensationlist	Perseverence	Intonation
Tolerate	Toxic	Law	Dark	Love
Toleration	Toxicity	Lawful	Darkly	Lover
Tolerance	Toxin	Lawfully	Darken	Loveable
Tolerant	Toxicology	Lawless	Darkness	Beloved
Tolerable	Detoxification	Lawlessly	Light	Unloved
Intolerable	Intoxicate	Unlawful	Lighten	Loveless
Intolerance	Intoxication	Unlawfully	Lighting	Loving
Intolerant	Intoxicant	Lawyer	Lighter	Lovingly
.	.	.	.	.
.	.	.	.	.
.	.	.	.	.

Logic List English: Meaningful Words - Volume 3

Acquire	Add	Advance	Affection	Betray
Acquisition	Addition	Advancement	Affectionate	Betrayal
Acquisitive	Additional	Advantage	Affectionately	Betrayer
Acquisitiveness	Additionally	Advantageous	Disaffected	Traitor
Require	Additive	Vantage	Disaffection	Traitorous
Requirement	Addendum	Disadvantage	Affected	Treachery
Requisite	Subtract	Disadvantageous	Unaffected	Treacherous
Requisition	Subtraction	Disadvantaged	Affecting	Treacherously
Forest	Arm	Aural	Friend	Four
Forested	Arms	Audible	Friendly	Fourth
Forestry	Armament	Audibly	Friendliness	Fourthly
Forester	Disarm	Audibility	Friendship	Foursome
Afforest	Unarmed	Auditory	Friendless	Fourteen
Afforestation	Armour	Inaudible	Befriend	Fourteenth
Deforest	Armoury	Audience	Unfriend	Forty
Deforestation	Armourer	Auditorium	Unfriendly	Fortieth
Nourish	Medicine	Drama	Military	Move
Nourishment	Medic	Dramatic	Militarism	Movement
Nourishing	Medical	Dramatically	Militarist	Moveable
Nutitious	Medically	Dramatize	Militant	Motion
Nutrition	Medicate	Dramatization	Militia	Remove
Nutrient	Medication	Dramatist	Paramilitary	Removal
Malnourished	Medicinal	Melodrama	Demilitarize	Removeable
Malnutrition	Premedication	Melodramatic	Demilitarization	Removers
Mutate	Ride	Thick	Deceive	Connect
Mutation	Rider	Thicken	Deceiver	Connection
Mutant	Riden	Thickly	Deceit	Connective
Mutable	Riding	Thickness	Deceitful	Connectivity
Transmute	Drive	Thin	Deception	Unconnected
Transmutation	Driver	Thinning	Deceptive	Disconnect
Transmogrify	Driven	Thinned	Deceptively	Disconnected
Immutable	Driving	Thinness	Deceptiveness	Reconnect
Penal	Assume	Private	Sacred	Conserve
Penalize	Assumption	Privately	Sacrosant	Conservation
Penalty	Presume	Privacy	Sanctify	Conservationist
Penance	Presumably	Privatize	Sanctity	Conservancy
Penitent	Presumption	Privatization	Consecrate	Preserve
Penitence	Presumptive	Public	Consecration	Preservation
Penitentiary	Presumptious	Publically	Sacrilege	Preservative
Penology	Presumptiously	Privy	Sacrilegious	Conservative

.	.	.	.	.
.	.	.	.	.
.	.	.	.	.

Serve	Succeed	Vacant	Visual	Economy
Service	Success	Vacancy	Visually	Economics
Servant	Successful	Vacate	Visualize	Economist
Servitude	Successfully	Evacuate	Visionary	Economic
Subservient	Succession	Vacuous	Vision	Economical
Subservience	Successive	Vacuum	Envision	Economize
Servile	Successively	Vacation	Envisage	Uneconomical
Servility	Successor	.	.	.
Oblige	Olfactory	Office	Optic	Oral
Obliging	Odour	Officer	Optics	Orally
Obligingly	Odourless	Officiate	Optical	Orator
Disobliging	Deodorize	Official	Optician	Oration
Obligate	Deodorization	Officialdom	Optometrist	Oratorio
Obligation	Odious	Unofficial	Ophthalmic	Aural
Obligatory	Odium	Officious	Ophthalmology	Aurally
Origin	Ova	Male	Reject	Pathos
Original	Ovary	Female	Rejection	Pathetic
Originally	Ovarian	Feminine	Eject	Sympathy
Originate	Ovulate	Femininity	Ejection	Sympathetic
Originator	Ovulation	Feminism	Ejector	Sympathize
Originality	Oval	Feminist	Inject	Sympathizer
Unoriginal	Ovoid	Effeminate	Injection	Empathy
Ensure	Envelop	Exhibit	Communicate	Impel
Insure	Envelopment	Exhibition	Communication	Impulse
Insurance	Envelope	Exhibitor	Communicative	Impulsive
Assure	Develop	Exhibitionist	Communique	Compel
Assuredly	Development	Exhibitionism	Communicable	Compulsion
Assurance	Developer	Inhibited	Communion	Compulsive
Reassure	Underdeveloped	Inhibition	Excommunicate	Compulsory
Export	Gentle	Gleam	Govern	Guard
Exporter	Gently	Gleaming	Governor	Guarded
Import	Gentleness	Glimmer	Governable	Guardedly
Importer	Gentleman	Gloom	Government	Guards
Importation	Genteel	Gloomy	Governmental	Ungarded
Deport	Gentry	Gloomily	Governess	Guardian
Deportation	Gentrify	Gloaming	Ungovernable	Guardianship
.	.	.	.	.
.	.	.	.	.
.	.	.	.	.
.	.	.	.	.
.	.	.	.	.
.	.	.	.	.

History	Horror	Ice	Luminous	Illusion
Historian	Horrible	Icy	Luminosity	Illusory
Historic	Horribly	Iciness	Luminescent	Delude
Historical	Horrify	Icycle	Luminescence	Deluded
Historically	Horrific	De-ice	Illuminate	Delusion
Prehistoric	Horrendous	Iced	Illumination	Disillusion
Prehistory	Horrid	Icing	Illuminating	Disillusionment
Perfect	Empire	Persona	Pragmatic	Fresh
Perfectly	Emperor	Personality	Pragmatist	Freshly
Perfection	Empress	Personify	Practical	Freshness
Perfectionist	Imperial	Personification	Practicable	Freshen
Perfectionism	Imperialism	Impersonate	Practicability	Refresh
Imperfect	Imperialist	Impersonation	Impractical	Refreshing
Imperfection	Imperious	Impersonator	Impracticable	Afresh
Animate	Breed	Accident	Cohere	Define
Animated	Breeding	Accidental	Cohesion	Definable
Inanimate	Breeder	Accidentally	Cohesive	Definition
Animal	Inborn	Incident	Coherent	Definite
Animator	Inbred	Incidental	Coherence	Definitely
Animation	Inbreeding	Incidentally	Incoherent	Indefinite
Animism	Interbreed	Incidence	Incoherence	Indefinitely
Dominate	Stable	Marry	Loose	Back
Domination	Stability	Marriage	Loosely	Backwards
Domineering	Stabilize	Matrimony	Loosen	Aback
Dominant	Stabilization	Matrimonial	Looseness	Backer
Dominance	Stabilizer	Intermarry	Tight	Backing
Dominion	Unstable	Intermarriage	Tighten	Backward
Indomitable	Instability	Unmarried	Tightly	Backwardness
Normal	Company	Amity	Chronology	Ascend
Normally	Companion	Amiable	Chronological	Ascension
Normality	Accompany	Amiably	Chronologically	Ascent
Normalize	Companionship	Amiability	Anachronism	Descend
Subnormal	Unaccompanied	Amicable	Chronicle	Descent
Abnormal	Accompanist	Amicably	Chronicler	Ascendant
Abnormality	Accompaniment	Amenable	Chronometer	Ascendancy
Arrange	Astronomy	Atheism	Belief	Fame
Rearrange	Astronomer	Atheist	Believe	Famed
Rearrangement	Astrophysics	Atheistic	Believer	Famous
Disarrange	Astrophysicist	Agnostic	Believable	Famously
Disarrangement	Astronaut	Agnostcism	Unbelievable	Infamy
Arrangement	Astronautics	Theology	Disbelief	Infamous
Prearranged	Astronomical	Theologian	Disbeliever	Infamously

Form	Fortune	Five	Frantic	Man
Format	Fortunate	Fifth	Frantically	Manly
Formation	Fortunately	Fiver	Frenetic	Manliness
Formative	Fortuitous	Fifteen	Frenetically	Manhood
Formless	Unfortunate	Fifteenth	Frenzy	Mannish
Deform	Unfortunately	Fifty	Frenzied	Masculine
Deformity	Misfortune	Fiftieth	Frenzedly	Masculinity
Mobile	Money	Rebel	Conciliate	Constituent
Mobility	Monied	Rebellion	Conciliation	Constituency
Mobilize	Monetary	Rebellious	Conciliatory	Constitution
Mobilization	Monetarism	Revolt	Reconcile	Constitutional
Immobile	Remunerate	Revolution	Reconcilable	Constitute
Immobility	Remuneration	Revolutionary	Reconciliation	Reconstitute
Immobilize	Remunerative	Revolutionize	Irreconcilable	Reconstitution
Regent	Rely	Repeat	Repute	Respect
Regency	Reliable	Repeated	Reputable	Respectful
Regicide	Reliably	Repeatedly	Reputation	Respecter
Regal	Reliability	Repetition	Disrepute	Respectable
Regally	Reliant	Repetitive	Disreputable	Respectability
Regality	Reliance	Repititious	Reputed	Disrespect
Regalia	Unreliable	Repeater	Reputedly	Disrespectful
Restrict	Right	Temper	Terror	Code
Restriction	Rightly	Tempestuous	Terrorize	Decode
Restrictive	Righteous	Temperamental	Terrorist	Decoder
Constrict	Righteously	Temperamentally	Terrorism	Cipher
Constriction	Wrong	Intemperate	Terrify	Decipher
Constrictive	Wrongly	Temperance	Terrifying	Decipherable
Constrictor	Wrongfully	Temperate	Terrible	Indecipherable
Populate	Despair	Qualify	Pliant	Propose
Population	Desperate	Qualified	Pliancy	Proposal
Populous	Desperately	Qualification	Pliable	Proposition
Populace	Desperation	Disqualify	Pliability	Proponent
Repopulate	Despondent	Disqualified	Comply	Oppose
Depopulate	Despondently	Disqualification	Compliant	Opponent
Depopulation	Despondency	Unqualified	Compliancy	Opposition
Complete	Conscious	Separate	Six	Special
Completely	Consciously	Separately	Sixth	Especial
Completeness	Consciousness	Separation	Sextet	Specially
Completion	Subconscious	Separable	Sixteen	Specialist
Incomplete	Subconsciously	Inseparable	Sixteenth	Specialize
Compliment	Unconscious	Separatist	Sixty	Specialization
Complimentary	Unconsciously	Separatism	Sixtieth	Speciality
.	.	.	.	.

Sulk	Use	Employ	Jell	Minister
Sulky	Usage	Employment	Jelly	Ministerial
Sulkily	Usable	Employer	Gel	Ministry
Sulkiness	Useful	Employee	Gelatin	Administrate
Sullen	Useless	Unemployed	Gelatine	Administration
Sullenly	Reuse	Unemployment	Gelatinous	Administrative
Sullenness	Misuse	Redeploy	Gelignite	Administrator
Vilify	West	Will	Wild	Woman
Vilification	Westerly	Wilful	Wildly	Womanly
Villain	Westward	Willing	Wildness	Womanhood
Villainous	Western	Willingly	Wilds	Womanish
Vindictive	Westerner	Willingness	Wilderness	Womb
Vile	Westernize	Unwilling	Bewilder	Womaniser
Wit	Worth	Night	Revert	Occupy
Witty	Worthy	Nightly	Reverse	Occupier
Wittily	Worthiness	Overnight	Reversal	Occupant
Witticism	Worthwhile	Nocturne	Reversion	Preoccupied
Wittingly	Worthless	Nocturnal	Reversible	Occupation
Witless	Unworthy	Fortnight	Irreversible	Occupational
Orient	Ego	Battle	Know	Courage
Orientation	Egotism	Batter	Knowledge	Courageous
Orienteering	Egotist	Embattled	Knowledgeable	Encourage
Disorient	Egotistic	Battery	Unknown	Encouragement
Disorientate	Egotistical	Battalion	Renowned	Discourage
Disorientation	Egocentric	Battlement	Acknowledge	Discouragement
Dear	Large	Light	Slave	Escape
Dearly	Largish	Lighten	Slavery	Escapee
Dearest	Enlarge	Enlighten	Slaver	Escapology
Endear	Enlargement	Enlightenment	Slavish	Escapologist
Endearing	Largely	Lightly	Enslave	Inescapable
Endearment	Largesse	Lightness	Enslavement	Escapism
Vapour	Exact	Execute	Inhale	Spend
Vaporize	Exactly	Execution	Inhalation	Expend
Vaporizer	Exacting	Executioner	Inhalent	Expenditure
Vaporous	Exactness	Prosecute	Inhaler	Expense
Evaporate	Exactitude	Prosecution	Exhale	Expensive
Evaporation	Inexact	Prosecutioner	Exhalation	Expendable

Expire	Explain	Explode	Expound	Interior
Expiry	Explanation	Explosion	Exposition	Internal
Expiration	Explanatory	Explosive	Express	Internally
Inspire	Explicable	Implode	Expression	Exterior
Inspiration	Unexplained	Implosion	Expressive	External
Inspirational	Inexplicable	Implosive	Expressionless	Externally
Intrude	Gamble	Avenge	Gender	Geology
Intruder	Gambling	Avenger	Genital	Geologist
Intrusion	Gambler	Revenge	Genitalia	Geological
Intrusive	Game	Vengeful	Generate	Geography
Extrude	Gaming	Vengeance	Generation	Geographical
Extrusion	Gamely	Vendetta	Genesis	Geographer
Glass	Glory	Graph	Grain	Grand
Glassy	Glorify	Graphics	Grainy	Grandly
Glassiness	Glorification	Graphology	Granule	Grandeur
Glaze	Glorious	Graphite	Granulate	Grandiose
Glazier	Gloriously	Graphic	Granulation	Aggrandise
Unglazed	Inglorious	Graphically	Granary	Aggrandisement
Green	Grumble	Habit	Habitat	Head
Greens	Grumbling	Habitual	Habitation	Header
Greenery	Grumbler	Habitually	Inhabit	Heads
Greenness	Grumpy	Habitue	Inhabitant	Behead
Greeny	Grumpily	Habituate	Uninhabitable	Heady
Greenish	Grumpiness	Habituation	Cohabit	Heading
Heart	Herb	Heredity	Hero	Hesitate
Hearten	Herbal	Hereditary	Heroic	Hesitation
Hearty	Herbalist	Heritage	Heroism	Hesitant
Dishearten	Herbaceous	Inherit	Heroics	Hesitantly
Heartily	Herbivore	Inheritor	Heroine	Hesitancy
Heartless	Herbicide	Inheritance	Anti-hero	Unhesitatingly
Honour	Theory	Logical	Immune	Politics
Honourable	Theorist	Logically	Immunity	Political
Honorary	Theoretical	Illogical	Immunize	Politically
Honorific	Theorize	Illogicality	Immunization	Politician
Dishonour	Hypothesis	Logistics	Immunology	Politic
Dishonourable	Hypothetical	Logistical	Immunologist	Impolitic
Potent	Pregnant	Radiate	Redeem	Calculate
Potency	Pregancy	Radiator	Redeemer	Calculation
Impotence	Impregnate	Radiation	Redeemable	Calculator
Impotent	Impregnation	Radium	Redemption	Calculus
Impotently	Impregnable	Irradiate	Redemptive	Calculating
Potentate	Impregnability	Irradiation	Irredeemable	Incalculable

Communicate	Compare	Corpse	Determine	Discreet
Communicative	Comparable	Corporal	Determinate	Discretion
Communication	Comparability	Corporeal	Indeterminate	Discretionary
Communique	Comparison	Incorporeal	Determinism	Indiscreet
Incommunicado	Comparative	Corpulent	Predetermined	Indiscreetly
Communicable	Incomparable	Corpulence	Determined	Indiscretion
Dispense	Industrial	Erase	Firm	Inject
Dispenser	Industrialize	Erasure	Firmly	Injection
Dispensary	Industrialization	Eraser	Firmness	Projectile
Dispensation	Industry	Eradicate	Infirm	Project
Dispensible	Indolent	Eradication	Infirmity	Projection
Indispensable	Indolence	Ineradicable	Infirmary	Projector
Initiate	Scribe	Sincere	Somnolence	Timid
Initiator	Scribble	Sincerely	Somnolent	Timidity
Initiation	Script	Sincerity	Soporific	Timorous
Initial	Scripture	Insincere	Insomnia	Intimidate
Initially	Inscribe	Insincerely	Insomniac	Intimidating
Initiative	Inscription	Insincerity	Somnambulist	Intimidation
Valid	Liberty	Like	Liquid	Advice
Validate	Liberate	Liken	Liquidize	Advise
Validation	Liberation	Likeness	Liquidizer	Adviser
Validity	Liberator	Likewise	Liquefy	Advisible
Invalid	Liberarian	Alike	Liquor	Advisability
Invalidate	Libertine	Unlike	Liquer	Inadvisable
Abstain	Access	Account	Admire	Verify
Abstainer	Accessible	Accounting	Admirable	Verfiable
Abstention	Accessibility	Accountant	Admirer	Verification
Abstinence	Inaccessible	Accountancy	Admiring	Veritable
Abstinent	Accede	Discount	Admiringly	Veracity
Abstemious	Accession	Unaccountable	Admiration	Veracious
Aggression	Chemist	Alternate	Anaesthesia	Appear
Aggressive	Chemistry	Alternation	Anaesthetic	Appearance
Aggressively	Chemical	Alternately	Anaesthetize	Disappear
Aggressiveness	Chemically	Alternator	Anaesthetist	Disappearance
Aggressor	Alchemy	Alternative	Analgesia	Reappear
Non-aggression	Alchemist	Alternatively	Analgesic	Reappearance
Arithmetic	Arrogance	Beauty	Late	Brute
Arithmetrical	Arrogant	Beautiful	Latish	Brutal
Mathematics	Humble	Beautify	Lateness	Brutally
Mathematician	Humbly	Beautician	Belated	Brutality
Mathematical	Humility	Ugly	Belatedly	Brutalize
Mathematically	Humiliate	Ugliness	Lately	Brutish

Fabricate	Favourable	Faith	Fool	Freeze
Fabrication	Favourably	Faithful	Foolish	Freezer
Fabricator	Unfavourable	Faithfulness	Foolishly	Frigid
Prefabricated	Favour	Fidelity	Foolishness	Refrigerate
Prefabrication	Favourite	Faithless	Foolery	Refrigeration
Fabric	Favouritism	Unfaithful	Folly	Refrigerator
Manage	Mechanic	Menopause	Method	Modify
Manager	Mechanical	Menopausal	Methodical	Modifier
Management	Mechanically	Menstruate	Methodically	Modification
Managerial	Mechanism	Menstruation	Methodology	Modulate
Mismanage	Mechanize	Menstrual	Methodism	Modulation
Mismanagement	Mechanization	Premenstrual	Methodist	Modulator
Music	Mute	Receive	Discover	Regress
Musical	Mutely	Receiver	Discovery	Regression
Musically	Muted	Reception	Discoverable	Regressive
Musician	Muffle	Receptive	Uncover	Progress
Musicology	Muffled	Receptivity	Undiscovered	Progression
Musicologist	Mutter	Recipient	Cover	Progressive
Related	Pay	Replica	Unite	Romance
Relation	Payable	Replicate	Union	Romantic
Relationship	Payment	Replication	Unity	Romantically
Relative	Repay	Duplicate	Unify	Romanticism
Interrelated	Repayment	Duplication	Unification	Romantize
Interrelationship	Repayable	Duplicator	Reunite	Romanticist
Rude	Three	Tolerate	Devil	Differ
Rudely	Third	Toleration	Devilish	Different
Rudeness	Thirteen	Tolerant	Devilry	Differently
Polite	Thirteenth	Tolerance	Devilment	Difference
Politely	Thirty	Tolerable	Diabolic	Differentiate
Politeness	Thirtieth	Tolerably	Diabolical	Indifference
Colour	Discriminate	Place	Distinct	Disturb
Colourless	Discrimination	Replace	Distinctly	Disturbing
Colourful	Discriminating	Replacement	Distinctive	Disturbed
Colourfully	Discriminatory	Displace	Distinctiveness	Perturb
Discolour	Indiscriminate	Displacement	Distinction	Disturbance
Discoloration	Indiscriminately	Misplace	Indistinct	Undisturbed
Dress	Drunk	Parson	Photograph	Pomp
Undress	Drunken	Parsonage	Photographic	Pompous
Undressing	Drunkenness	Parish	Photography	Pompously
Dressy	Drunkard	Parishioner	Photographer	Pomposity
Dressily	Sober	Pastor	Photogenic	Pontificate
Dresser	Sobriety	Pastoral	Unphotogenic	Pontification

Caution	Principal	Proscribe	Punch	Character
Cautious	Principally	Proscription	Pugnacious	Characterise
Cautiously	Prime	Proscriptive	Pugnacity	Characterization
Cautionary	Primary	Prohibit	Pugilism	Characteristic
Precaution	Primarily	Prohibition	Pugilist	Characteristically
Precautionary	Primate	Prohibitive	Pugilistic	Uncharacteristic
Certain	Clean	Cognizance	Colony	Collect
Certainty	Cleanliness	Cognizant	Colonist	Collection
Certitude	Cleaner	Cognitive	Colonize	Collector
Certainly	Cleanse	Cognition	Colonization	Collectively
Uncertain	Cleanser	Cogitate	Colonial	Recollect
Uncertainty	Unclean	Cogitation	Colonialism	Recollection
Compare	Confide	Congregate	Contract	Courtesy
Comparable	Confidant	Congregation	Contractor	Courteous
Comparative	Confidence	Segregate	Contractual	Courteously
Comparatively	Confidential	Segregation	Subcontract	Discourteous
Comparison	Confidentially	Desegregate	Subcontractor	Discourteously
Incomparable	Confidentiality	Disegregation	Contraction	Discourtesy
Critic	Culture	Cut	Sequel	Sadist
Criticism	Cultured	Cutter	Sequence	Sadism
Criticize	Cultural	Cutting	Sequential	Sadistic
Critical	Cultivated	Uncut	Prequel	Masochist
Uncritical	Cultivate	Cutlass	Subsequent	Masochism
Critically	Cultivation	Cutlery	Subsequently	Masochistic
Secret	Select	Self	Seven	Sex
Secretly	Selection	Selfish	Seventh	Sexual
Secrecy	Selective	Selfishly	Seventeen	Sexually
Secretive	Selectively	Selfishness	Seventeenth	Sexuality
Secretiveness	Selectivity	Selfless	Seventy	Sexist
Secrete	Selector	Unselfish	Seventieth	Sexism
Sick	Silence	Simple	Sleep	Slow
Sicken	Silent	Simply	Sleeper	Slowly
Sickness	Silently	Simplify	Sleepy	Slowness
Sickly	Noise	Simplification	Sleepily	Quick
Ill	Noisy	Simplicity	Sleepiness	Quickly
Illness	Noisily	Simplistic	Sleepless	Quicken
Soft	Spirit	Stupor	Style	Suppose
Soften	Spiritual	Stupefy	Stylish	Supposition
Hard	Spiritually	Stupefaction	Stylishly	Supposed
Harden	Spirituality	Stupid	Stylist	Supposedly
Hardness	Spiritualism	Stupidly	Stylize	Presuppose
Hardly	Spiritualist	Stupidity	Stylistic	Presupposition

Logic List English: Meaningful Words - Volume 3

Kind	Quiet	Quote	Vegan	Vigil
Kindly	Quieten	Quotation	Vegetable	Vigilant
Kindliness	Quietly	Quotable	Vegetarian	Vigilance
Kindness	Quietism	Misquote	Vegetation	Vigilante
Unkind	Quiescent	Misquotation	Vegetate	Invigilator
Violate	Weak	Eat	Educate	Face
Violation	Weakly	Eatable	Education	Facade
Inviolate	Weaken	Edible	Educational	Fascia
Violence	Weakness	Edibility	Educative	Deface
Violent	Weakling	Inedible	Coeducation	Facing
Word	Write	Navigate	Nerve	Noble
Wordy	Writer	Navigation	Neural	Nobly
Wording	Writing	Navigable	Neuralgia	Nobility
Byword	Written	Navigator	Neuritis	Nobleman
Watchword	Rewrite	Unnavigable	Neurology	Ignoble
Node	North	Nude	Operate	Opportunity
Nodule	Northern	Nudity	Operation	Opportunist
Noddle	Northerly	Nudism	Operational	Opportune
Noggin	Northwards	Naked	Operator	Opportunism
Nod	Northener	Nakedness	Operative	Inopportune
Order	Organise	Front	Elect	Mend
Orderly	Organiser	Frontal	Election	Amend
Orderliness	Organization	Frontage	Electoral	Amends
Disorder	Disorganised	Affront	Electorate	Amendment
Disorderliness	Reorganisation	Effrontary	Electable	Emend
Eminent	Power	Camp	Enchant	Feeble
Eminently	Powerful	Camper	Enchantment	Feebly
Eminence	Empower	Encamp	Enchantress	Feebleness
Pre-eminent	Disempower	Encampment	Disenchant	Enfeeble
Pre-eminence	Powerless	Decamp	Disenchantment	Enfeeblement
Engage	Rich	Sign	Enthuse	Diagram
Engaged	Richly	Signal	Enthusiasm	Diagramatic
Engagement	Richness	Signify	Enthusiast	Monogram
Engaging	Riches	Ensign	Enthusiastic	Anagram
Disengage	Enrich	Insignia	Enthusiastically	Epigram
Esteem	Event	Exceed	Except	Exhaust
Estimable	Non-event	Exceedingly	Exception	Exhaustive
Estimate	Eventual	Excel	Exceptionable	Exhaustion
Estimation	Eventually	Excellent	Exceptional	Exhaustible
Inestimable	Eventing	Excellence	Unexceptional	Inexhaustible
.	.	.	.	.
.	.	.	.	.

25

Imply	Impose	Impressionism	Extent	Gastric
Implicit	Imposition	Impressionist	Extensive	Gastritis
Implicitly	Expose	Impressionistic	Extend	Gastronomic
Explicit	Exposure	Expression	Extendible	Gastronomy
Explicitly	Exposition	Expressionist	Extension	Gastropod
General	Glob	Gyrate	Heal	Honest
Generally	Globule	Gyration	Health	Honesty
Generalize	Globe	Gyratory	Healthy	Honestly
Generalization	Global	Gyroscope	Healthily	Dishonest
Generality	Globally	Autogyro	Unhealthy	Dishonestly
Cultivate	Host	Hot	Human	Humid
Cultivation	Hostess	Hotly	Humanity	Humidity
Horticulture	Hospitable	Hotish	Humanize	Humidify
Horticultural	Hospitality	Heat	Humanism	Humidifier
Horticulturalist	Inhospitable	Heater	Humanly	Dehumidify
Hypnosis	Identity	Ignore	Imitate	Patience
Hypnotic	Identify	Ignorance	Imitation	Patient
Hypnotize	Identifiable	Ignorant	Imitative	Patiently
Hypnotism	Identification	Ignorantly	Imitator	Impatient
Hypnotist	Identical	Ignoramus	Inimitable	Impatiently
Perceive	Pertain	Placid	Plant	Proper
Perception	Pertinent	Placidity	Planter	Properly
Perceptive	Pertinence	Placate	Plantation	Improper
Perceptible	Impertinent	Implacable	Implant	Propriety
Imperceptible	Impertinence	Implacability	Implantation	Impropriety
Repair	Resist	Irritate	Accurate	Adequate
Repairable	Resistant	Irritation	Accuracy	Adequately
Reparation	Resistable	Irritant	Accurately	Adequacy
Irreparable	Irresistible	Irritable	Inaccurate	Inadequate
Disrepair	Irresistably	Irritably	Inaccuracy	Inadequacy
Articulate	Cease	Conclude	Decent	Delicate
Articulation	Ceaseless	Conclusion	Decency	Delicately
Inarticulate	Cessation	Conclusive	Indecent	Delicacy
Articulated	Incessant	Conclusively	Indeceny	Indelicate
Articulation	Unceasing	Inconclusive	Indecently	Indelicacy
Describe	Dispose	Doctrine	Induce	Apt
Description	Disposable	Doctrinal	Inducement	Aptly
Descriptive	Disposal	Doctrinaire	Induct	Aptness
Indescribable	Disposition	Indoctrinate	Induction	Aptitude
Indescribably	Indisposed	Indoctrination	Inductance	Ineptitude
.	.	.	.	.
.	.	.	.	.

Fatuous	Infect	Infinite	Fluent	Sane
Fatuously	Infectious	Infinity	Fluency	Sanity
Infatuate	Infection	Finite	Fluently	Insane
Infatuated	Disinfect	Infinitely	Influence	Insanely
Infatuation	Disinfectant	Infinitesimal	Influential	Insanity
Significant	Solve	Inspect	Suffer	Integrity
Significantly	Solvable	Inspection	Suffering	Integrate
Significance	Solution	Inspector	Sufferer	Integration
Insignificant	Soluble	Introspect	Sufferance	Disintegrate
Insignificance	Insoluble	Introspection	Insufferable	Disintegration
Change	Interest	Lancet	Last	Liberal
Changeable	Interesting	Lanceolate	Lastly	Liberally
Unchanging	Interestingly	Lance	Latter	Liberality
Interchange	Disinterest	Lancer	Latterly	Liberalize
Interchangeable	Disinterested	Freelance	Lately	Liberalization
Alone	Loyal	Lucid	Luck	Luxury
Lonely	Loyally	Lucidly	Lucky	Luxurious
Lonliness	Loyalty	Lucidity	Luckily	Luxuriant
Lonesome	Loyalist	Elucidate	Luckless	Luxuriance
Lone	Disloyal	Elucidation	Unlucky	Luxuriate
Lofty	Base	Abolish	Absolute	Absorb
Loftily	Basely	Abolition	Absolutely	Absorption
Loftiness	Baseness	Abolishinist	Absolutism	Absorbant
Aloof	Abase	Demolish	Absolve	Absorbency
Aloofness	Abasement	Demolition	Absolution	Malabsorption
Abuse	Cumulative	Accuse	Adequate	Adjust
Abusive	Accumlate	Accused	Adequately	Adjustment
Abusively	Accumulation	Accuser	Adequacy	Adjustable
Abusiveness	Accumulative	Accusing	Inadequate	Readjust
Disabuse	Accumulator	Accusation	Inadequacy	Readjustment
Admit	Mix	Adore	Aerate	Aerial
Admittedly	Mixed	Adorable	Aeration	Aeroplane
Admissible	Mixture	Adoration	Aerosol	Aerobatic
Admissibility	Mixer	Adoring	Aerobic	Aerobatics
Inadmissible	Admixture	Adoringly	Aerobics	Aerodrome
Aerospace	Confirm	Fix	Fix	Flame
Aeronautics	Confirmation	Fixative	Fixed	Flammable
Aeronautical	Affirm	Fixture	Fixedly	Inflammable
Aerodynamic	Affirmation	Affix	Fixation	Aflame
Aerodynamics	Affirmative	Fixer	Fixated	Flambe
.	.	.	.	.
.	.	.	.	.

Ambivalent	Mid	Analyse	Anarchy	Antagonize
Ambivalence	Middle	Analyst	Anarchic	Antagonism
Ambiguous	Midst	Analytic	Anarchism	Antagonist
Ambiguously	Amid	Analytical	Anarchist	Antagonistic
Ambiguity	Amidst	Analysis	Anarchistic	Protagonist
Apathy	Proximity	Argue	Atom	Astute
Apathetic	Proximate	Argument	Atomic	Astutely
Pathetic	Approximate	Argumentative	Atomize	Astuteness
Pathetically	Approximately	Arguable	Subatomic	Shrewd
Pathos	Approximation	Arguably	Atomizer	Shrewdly
Authority	Biography	Bag	Barbarian	Base
Authorize	Biographical	Bagged	Barbaric	Basic
Authorization	Biographer	Bagging	Barbarism	Basics
Authorative	Autobiography	Baggage	Barbarity	Basically
Authoritarian	Autobiographical	Baggy	Barbarous	Basis
Fit	Bid	Biology	Break	Breath
Fitting	Bidding	Biologist	Breakable	Breathless
Fitness	Biddable	Biological	Breakage	Breathe
Befit	Forbid	Microbiology	Broken	Breathing
Befitting	Forbidden	Microbiologist	Unbreakable	Breathalyze
Fair	Familiar	Fault	Fiction	Fierce
Fairly	Familiarity	Faulty	Fictional	Fiercely
Fairness	Familiarize	Faultily	Fictionalize	Fierceness
Unfair	Familiarization	Faultless	Fictitious	Ferocity
Unfairly	Unfamiliar	Faultlessly	Non-fiction	Ferocious
Flat	Finance	Formal	Fright	Frost
Inflate	Financial	Fomally	Frighten	Frosty
Inflation	Financially	Formality	Frightening	Frostiness
Inflatable	Financier	Informal	Frightful	Frostbite
Deflate	Fiscal	Informality	Afraid	Frostbitten
Fruit	Mad	Magnet	Maternal	Mature
Fruitful	Madly	Magnetic	Maternity	Maturity
Fruition	Madness	Magnetically	Motherly	Immature
Fructify	Madden	Magnetism	Matriarch	Immaturity
Fruitless	Maddening	Magnetize	Matriarchy	Premature
Maximum	Measure	Minute	Melody	Microbe
Maximize	Measured	Minutely	Melodic	Microscope
Minimum	Measurable	Miniscule	Melodious	Microscopy
Minimal	Measurement	Miniature	Mellow	Microscopic
Minimize	Immeasurable	Miniaturize	Melifluous	Microscopically
.	.	.	.	.
.	.	.	.	.

Understand	Modern	Monk	Mount	Multiple
Understanding	Modernize	Monkish	Mountain	Multiplicity
Understandable	Modernization	Monastic	Mountainous	Multitude
Understandably	Modernism	Monasticism	Mountineer	Multitudinous
Misunderstand	Modernist	Monastry	Mountineering	Multiply
React	Read	Reason	Reciprocal	Commend
Reaction	Reader	Reasonable	Reciprocally	Commendable
Reactive	Reading	Reasonably	Reciprococity	Commendation
Reactionary	Readable	Unreasonable	Reciprocate	Recommend
Reactor	Readership	Unreasonably	Reciprocation	Recommendation
Construct	Occur	Refine	Inflate	Relax
Construction	Occurrence	Refined	Inflation	Relaxing
Constructive	Recur	Refinement	Inflationary	Relaxation
Reconstruct	Recurrence	Refinery	Deflate	Tense
Reconstruction	Recurrent	Unrefined	Deflation	Tension
Demonstrate	Respond	Responsible	Rough	Think
Demonstration	Response	Responsibly	Roughly	Thinking
Demonstrator	Responsive	Responsibility	Roughen	Thinker
Remonstrate	Responsiveness	Irresponsible	Roughness	Rethink
Remonstration	Unresponsive	Irresponsibility	Rugged	Thoughtless
Torture	Transition	Truth	Dead	Accelerate
Torturer	Transitional	Truly	Deadly	Acceleration
Torment	Transitory	Truism	Deaden	Accelerator
Tormentor	Transient	Untruth	Death	Decelerate
Tortuous	Transcience	Untruthful	Deathly	Deceleration
Decide	Decorate	Deduce	Deep	Defeat
Decision	Decoration	Deducible	Deeply	Defeatist
Decided	Decorator	Deduction	Deepen	Defeatism
Decisive	Decorative	Deductive	Shallow	Undefeated
Decisiveness	Decor	Deduct	Shallowness	Undefatigable
Hydrate	Depress	Deprive	Deride	Desire
Hydration	Depression	Deprived	Derision	Desirable
Dehydrate	Depressive	Deprivation	Derisive	Desirability
Dehydration	Depressingly	Depraved	Derisory	Desirous
Rehydrate	Anti-depressant	Depravity	Dergatory	Undesirable
Destroy	Devotee	Proportion	Content	Interupt
Destroyer	Devotion	Proportionate	Contented	Interuption
Destructive	Devotional	Proportional	Contentment	Disrupt
Destruction	Devout	Disproportion	Discontent	Disruption
Indestructable	Devoutly	Disproportionate	Discontentment	Disruptive
.	.	.	.	.
.	.	.	.	.

Similar	Soluble	Distil	Contort	Divide
Similarly	Solubility	Distillation	Contortion	Division
Similarity	Solution	Distillate	Torsion	Subdivide
Similitude	Solvent	Distiller	Distort	Subdivision
Dissimilar	Dissolve	Distillery	Distortion	Divisive
Domestic	Dope	Doze	Draw	Duke
Domesticate	Dopey	Dozy	Drawing	Dukedom
Domestication	Dormant	Drowse	Draught	Ducal
Domesticity	Dormancy	Drowsy	Draughtsman	Duchy
Undomesticated	Dormitory	Drowsiness	Draughty	Duchess
Pack	Pope	Part	Paternal	Peace
Packet	Pontiff	Partly	Paternity	Peaceable
Package	Papal	Partial	Patriarch	Peaceably
Packaging	Papacy	Partially	Patriarchy	Peaceful
Prepacked	Papist	Particle	Patricide	Peacefully
Pervert	Pharmacy	Popular	Prefer	Prepare
Perversion	Pharmacist	Popularity	Preferable	Prepared
Perverse	Pharmacology	Popularly	Preferably	Preparation
Perversely	Pharmacologist	Popularize	Preference	Preparatory
Perversity	Pharmaceutical	Unpopular	Preferential	Unprepared
Prevent	Protect	Putrid	Cancer	Category
Preventable	Protection	Putrify	Cancerous	Categorize
Prevention	Protective	Putrification	Carcinogen	Categorization
Preventive	Protector	Putrefaction	Carcinogenic	Categorical
Unpreventable	Protectorate	Putrescent	Carcinoma	Categorically
Cause	Cave	Century	Censor	Certify
Causal	Cavern	Centenary	Censorship	Certifiable
Causality	Cavernous	Centennial	Uncensored	Certification
Causation	Caving	Centenarian	Censure	Certificate
Effect	Caver	Bicentenary	Censorious	Uncertificated
Civic	Comic	Compute	Conclude	Conduct
Civil	Comical	Computation	Conclusion	Conduction
Civilian	Comically	Computer	Conclusive	Conductive
Citizen	Comedy	Computerize	Conclusively	Conductor
Citizenship	Comedian	Computerization	Inconclusive	Conductivity
Federal	Consult	Converse	Control	Contaminate
Federation	Consultant	Conversation	Controller	Contamination
Confederate	Consultancy	Conversational	Controllable	Contaminant
Confederation	Consultation	Conversationalist	Uncontrolled	Decontaminate
Confederacy	Consultative	Conversant	Uncontrollable	Decontamination
.	.	.	.	.
.	.	.	.	.

Cool	Correct	Cryptic	Cube	Curt
Coolly	Correctly	Cryptically	Cubicle	Curtly
Coolness	Correction	Cryptogram	Cubic	Curtness
Coolant	Corrective	Crypography	Cubist	Curtail
Cooler	Correctness	Crypt	Cubism	Curtailment
Sage	School	Science	Sculpt	Section
Sagacity	Scholar	Scientific	Sculpture	Sectional
Sagacious	Scholarly	Scientifically	Sculptural	Sector
Sapient	Scholastic	Scientist	Sculptor	Subsection
Sapience	Scholarship	Unscientific	Sculptress	Segment
Seduce	Seismic	Sheep	Smoke	Solid
Seducer	Seismology	Shepherd	Smoky	Solidly
Seductress	Seismologist	Sherperdess	Smoker	Solidity
Seduction	Seismometer	Sheepish	Smokeless	Solidify
Seductive	Seismograph	Sheepishly	Smoulder	Solidarity
South	Spectacle	Speak	Statistic	Steady
Southern	Spectacular	Speaker	Statistics	Steadily
Southerly	Spectacularly	Speech	Statistical	Steadiness
Southwards	Spectate	Speechless	Statistically	Steadfast
Southerner	Spectator	Spokesman	Statistician	Steadfastness
Strange	Strategy	Strict	Suffice	Suit
Strangely	Stratagem	Strictly	Sufficient	Suitable
Strangeness	Strategic	Strictness	Sufficiently	Suitably
Stranger	Strategically	Lax	Sufficiency	Suitability
Estranged	Strategist	Laxity	Insufficient	Unsuitable
Sweet	System	Wood	Objective	Grief
Sweeten	Systemic	Wooden	Objectivity	Grieve
Sweetener	Systematic	Woody	Subject	Grievance
Sweetness	Systematically	Wooded	Subjective	Aggrieved
Sweetly	Systemization	Woods	Subjectivity	Grievous
Earth	Adventure	Visible	Virus	Volunteer
Earthy	Adventurous	Visibility	Viral	Voluntary
Unearth	Adventurer	Invisible	Virology	Voluntarily
Unearthly	Venture	Invisibility	Virulent	Involuntarily
Waste	Weary	Weigh	White	Wide
Waster	Wearily	Weight	Whitish	Width
Wastage	Wearisome	Weighty	Whiteness	Widely
Wastful	Weariness	Weightless	Whiting	Widen
.	.	.	.	.
.	.	.	.	.
.	.	.	.	.
.	.	.	.	.

East	Edge	Edit	Wire	Wise
Easterly	Edging	Editor	Wiring	Wisely
Eastern	Edgways	Edition	Wireless	Wisdom
Eastwards	Edgy	Editorial	Wiry	Unwise
Wonder	Wrest	Work	Youth	Wretch
Wondrous	Wrestle	Worker	Youthful	Wretched
Wonderment	Wrestler	Workman	Young	Wretchedly
Wonderful	Wrestling	Workable	Youngster	Wretchedness
Narrate	Narrow	Navy	Neighbour	Nice
Narrator	Narrows	Naval	Neighbouring	Niceness
Narration	Narrowness	Nautical	Neighbourhood	Nicely
Narrative	Narrowly	Nautilus	Neighbourly	Nicety
Nuclear	Nose	Object	Object	Join
Neutron	Nostril	Objection	Objective	Joint
Neutrino	Nosey	Objector	Purpose	Joiner
Nucleus	Nosiness	Objectionable	Purposefully	Joinery
Offend	Oil	One	Open	Obscene
Offender	Oily	Oneness	Openly	Obscenity
Offence	Ointment	Oneself	Opening	Obnoxious
Offensive	Oleaginous	Once	Unopened	Obnoxiousness
Orchestra	Organ	Ornament	Ostensible	Ordinary
Orchestrate	Organic	Ornamental	Ostensibly	Ordinarily
Orchestration	Organism	Ornamentation	Ostentation	Extraordinary
Orchestral	Inorganic	Ornate	Ostentatious	Extraordinarily
Rage	Overt	Own	Oxygen	Bitter
Outrage	Overtly	Owner	Oxygenate	Bitterness
Outrageous	Covert	Ownership	Oxide	Bitterly
Outrageously	Covertly	Disown	Oxidize	Embitter
Body	Bold	Emphasis	Place	Crust
Bodily	Boldly	Emphasize	Placement	Crusty
Embody	Boldness	Emphatic	Emplacement	Encrust
Embodiment	Embolden	Emphatically	Replace	Crustacean
End	Danger	Endure	Energy	Franchise
Ending	Dangerous	Endurable	Energize	Enfranchise
Endless	Dangerously	Endurance	Energetic	Enfranchisement
Endways	Endanger	Unendurable	Energetically	Disenfranchise
Engrave	Rapt	Tangle	Enter	Title
Engraver	Rapture	Entangle	Entry	Titled
Engraving	Rapturous	Entanglement	Entrance	Entitled
Graven	Enrapture	Disentangle	Entrant	Entitlement
.	.	.	.	.
.	.	.	.	.

Erode	Epidermis	Telegram	Distant	Environs
Erosion	Dermatitis	Telegraph	Distantly	Environment
Corrode	Dermatology	Telegraphic	Distance	Environmental
Corrosion	Dermatologist	Telegraphy	Equidistant	Environmentalist
Err	Ethics	Evangelism	Evidence	Evolve
Error	Ethical	Evangelist	Evident	Evolution
Erroneous	Ethically	Evangelize	Evidential	Evolutionary
Errant	Unethical	Evangelical	Evidently	Devolve
Exam	Excite	Exclaim	Excrete	Expand
Examination	Excitable	Exclamation	Excretion	Expansion
Examiner	Excitement	Exclamatory	Excreta	Expanse
Examine	Excitability	Declaim	Excrement	Expansive
Expect	Expedite	Experiment	Extinct	Extreme
Expectation	Expeditious	Experimental	Extinction	Extremely
Expectant	Expedition	Experimentation	Extinguish	Extremist
Expectancy	Expeditionary	Experimenter	Extinguisher	Extremity
Introvert	Ghost	Glad	God	Go
Introversion	Ghostly	Gladly	Godess	Going
Extrovert	Ghoul	Gladness	Godly	Gone
Extroversion	Ghoulish	Gladden	Ungodly	Goner
Good	Great	Greed	Quaver	Guilt
Goodly	Greater	Greedy	Quiver	Guilty
Goodly	Greatness	Greedily	Quake	Guiltily
Goodness	Greatly	Greediness	Earthquake	Guiltless
Gun	Gymnasium	Hallucinate	Hazard	Haste
Gunner	Gymnastics	Hallucination	Harzardous	Hasty
Gunnery	Gymnastic	Hallucinatory	Haphazard	Hastily
Gunman	Gymnast	Hallucinogen	Haphazardly	Posthaste
Heat	Heavy	High	Help	Hill
Heated	Heavily	Highly	Helper	Hilly
Heatedly	Heaviness	Height	Helpful	Hillock
Heater	Heave	Heighten	Unhelpful	Uphill
Hospital	Hotel	Idiot	Idle	Idol
Hospitalize	Hotelier	Idiocy	Idly	Idolatry
Hospitalization	Hostel	Idiotic	Idler	Idolater
Hospice	Hostelry	Idiotically	Idleness	Idolize
Palpable	Partial	Penetrate	Personal	Pervade
Palpably	Partiality	Penetration	Personally	Pervasive
Impalpable	Impartial	Penetrable	Impersonal	Pervious
Palpate	Impartiality	Impenetrable	Personable	Impervious
.	.	.	.	.
.	.	.	.	.

Ponderous	Poor	Prison	Isle	Isolate
Ponderously	Poverty	Prisoner	Islet	Isolation
Ponder	Impoverish	Imprison	Island	Isolationism
Imponderable	Impoverished	Imprisonment	Islander	Isolationist
Reduce	Refute	Relevant	Revoke	Auspices
Reducible	Refutable	Relevancy	Revocation	Auspicious
Reduction	Refutation	Irrelevant	Irrevocable	Auspiciously
Irreducible	Irrefutable	Irrelevance	Irrevocably	Inauspicious
Build	Congruent	Consequence	Constant	Continent
Builder	Congruence	Consequently	Constantly	Continence
Building	Incongruous	Consequential	Constancy	Incontinent
Rebuild	Incongruity	Inconsequential	Inconstant	Incontinence
Corporate	Corrupt	Increase	Curious	Debt
Corporation	Corruption	Increasingly	Curiously	Debtor
Incorporate	Corruptible	Increment	Curiosity	Indebted
Incorporation	Incorruptible	Decrease	Curio	Indebtedness
Indicate	Dignity	Dispute	Dissolve	Equity
Indicator	Dignitary	Disputation	Dissolution	Equitable
Indication	Undignified	Indisputable	Indissoluble	Equable
Indicative	Indignity	Indisputably	Dissolute	Inequitable
Fallible	Infant	Inferior	Inflame	Inflate
Fallibility	Infancy	Inferiority	Inflamed	Inflation
Infallible	Infantile	Superior	Inflammation	Inflationary
Infallibility	Infanticide	Superiority	Inflammatory	Deflation
Flux	Inflict	Fury	Innocence	Secure
Fluctuate	Infliction	Furious	Innocent	Securely
Fluctuation	Afflict	Furiously	Innocently	Security
Influx	Affliction	Infuriate	Innocuous.	Insecure
Inside	Solvent	Institute	Instruct	Instrument
Insider	Solvency	Institution	Instructor	Instrumental
Outside	Insolvent	Institutional	Instructive	Instrumentalist
Outsider	Insolvency	Institutionalize	Instruction	Instrumentation
Support	Intend	Interfere	Planet	Play
Supportive	Intention	Interfering	Planetary	Playful
Supporter	Intentional	Interference	Planetarium	Interplay
Insupportable	Intentionally	Interferon	Interplanetary	Player
Interpret	Interrogate	Dissect	Traction	IntuitionIntuitive
Interpretor	Interrogation	Dissection	Tractor	Intuitively
Interpretation	Interrogator	Bisect	Tractable	Tuition
Reinterpret	Interrogative	Intersect	Intractable	.
.	.	.	.	.
.	.	.	.	.

Invert	Investigate	Vigour	Invite	Vulnerable
Inversion	Investigation	Vigorous	Invitation	Vulnerability
Inverse	Investigator	Vigorously	Inviting	Invulnerable
Inversely	Investigative	Invigorate	Uninviting	Invulnerability
Languish	Laud	Laze	Lead	Learn
Langour	Laudable	Lazy	Leading	Learner
Languid	Laudably	Lazily	Leader	Learned
Languidly	Laudatory	Laziness	Leadership	Learning
Leg	Like	Limit	Liquidate	Low
Leggy	Liking	Limitation	Liquidator	Lower
Leggings	Likeable	Limitless	Liquidation	Lowly
Legless	Dislike	Unlimited	Liquidity	Lowliness
Loud	Long	Cosmic	Crafty	Crazed
Loudly	Longer	Cosmos	Craftiness	Crazy
Loudness	Longevity	Cosmology	Cunning	Crazily
Aloud	Prolong	Cosmonaut	Cunningly	Craziness
Create	Cross	Cross	Cure	Curve
Creative	Crossly	Crucify	Curable	Curvature
Creativity	Crossness	Crucifixion	Curative	Curvaceous
Creator	Crossing	Crucifix	Incurable	Curvy
Custom	Cynic	Cycle	Sad	Safe
Customary	Cynical	Cyclist	Sadly	Safely
Customarily	Cynically	Cycling	Sadness	Safety
Accustom	Cynicism	Bicycle	Sadden	Unsafe
Saint	Sale	Sarcasm	Satire	Save
Saintly	Saleable	Sarcastic	Satirize	Saver
Saintliness	Salesman	Sarcastically	Satirist	Saving
Sainthood	Salesmanship	Sardonic	Satirical	Savings
Scab	Scant	Scene	Sceptic	Scot
Scabby	Scanty	Scenic	Sceptical	Scotsman
Scales	Scantily	Scenery	Sceptically	Scottish
Scaley	Scantiness	Scenario	Scepticism	Scotch
Scruple	Seam	Season	Attach	Shallow
Scrupulous	Seamless	Seasonal	Attachment	Shallowness
Scrupulously	Seamstress	Seasonable	Detach	Shallows
Unscrupulous	Seamy	Seasoning	Detachment	Deep
Shade	Sharp	Sign	Complex	Single
Shady	Sharpen	Signature	Complexity	Singly
Shadow	Sharpener	Signatory	Complicate	Singular
Shadowy	Blunt	Signet	Complication	Singularly
.	.	.	.	.
.	.	.	.	.

Slack	Smart	Snob	Sociable	Sophisticate
Slacken	Smartly	Snobbish	Sociably	Sophisticated
Slackness	Smartness	Snobbery	Sociability	Sophistication
Slacker	Smarten	Snooty	Unsociable	Unsophisticated
Spark	Specific	Speculate	Splendid	Sterile
Sparkle	Specifically	Speculation	Splendidly	Sterilize
Sparkler	Specify	Speculative	Splendour	Sterilization
Sparkling	Specification	Speculator	Resplendent	Sterility
Stiff	Stigma	Stimulus	Stoic	Strangle
Stiffly	Stigmatize	Stimulate	Stoical	Strangler
Stiffen	Stigmatization	Stimulation	Stoically	Strangulation
Stiffness	Stigmata	Stimulant	Stoicism	Stranglehold
Stub	Study	Stump	Emerge	Substance
Stubby	Student	Stumpy	Emergence	Substantiate
Stubble	Studious	Stunt	Submerge	Substantiation
Stubbly	Studiously	Stunted	Submersion	Substantial
Suggest	Suicide	Supervise	Supreme	Surgeon
Suggestion	Suicidal	Supervisor	Supremely	Surgery
Suggestive	Suicidally	Supervisory	Supremacy	Surgical
Suggestively	Homicide	Supervision	Supremo	Surgically
Surreal	Survive	Suspect	Parasite	Symbol
Surrealist	Survival	Suspicion	Parasitic	Symbolic
Surrealistic	Survivor	Suspicious	Symbiosis	Symbolically
Surrealism	Revive	Suspiciously	Symbiotic	Symbolism
Synthesis	Brief	Blaze	Abominate	Abort
Synthesize	Briefly	Blazing	Abomination	Abortive
Synthetic	Abbreviate	Ablaze	Abominable	Abortion
Synthesizer	Abbreviation	Blazer	Abominably	Abortionist
Bounds	Accent	Accept	Climate	Accomplish
Boundary	Unaccented	Acceptable	Clime	Accomplished
Abound	Accentuate	Acceptability	Acclimatize	Accomplishment
Abounding	Accentuation	Unacceptable	Acclimatization	Accomplice
Acid	Acquaint	Act	Acute	Addict
Acidic	Acquainted	Acting	Acutely	Addicted
Acidity	Acquaintence	Actor	Acuteness	Addiction
Acidify	Unacquainted	Actress	Acuity	Addictive
Adult	Adroit	Drift	Advert	Aesthetic
Adulthood	Adroitly	Drifting	Advertising	Aesthetics
Adolescence	Adroitness	Adrift	Advertiser	Aesthetically
Adolescent	Maladroit	Drifter	Advertisement	Aesthete
.	.	.	.	.
.	.	.	.	.

Logic List English: Meaningful Words - Volume 3

Age	Air	Alien	Allege	Ally
Aging	Airy	Alienation	Alleged	Allied
Aged	Airiness	Alienate	Allegedly	Alliance
Ageless	Airless	Inalienable	Allegation	Allegiance
Allot	Relief	Allow	Might	Amaze
Allotment	Relieve	Allowance	Mighty	Amazing
Allocate	Alleviate	Allowable	Mightily	Amazingly
Allocation	Alleviation	Disallow	Almighty	Amazement
Dextrous	Ambition	Amour	Amplify	Note
Dextrously	Ambitious	Amorous	Amplifier	Notation
Dexterity	Ambitiously	Amorousness	Amplification	Annotate
Ambidextrous	Ambitiousness	Enamoured	Amplitude	Annotation
Annual	Antique	Appetite	Apply	Comprehend
Annually	Antiquarian	Appetizer	Applied	Comprehension
Annals	Antiquity	Appertizing	Appliance	Comprehensible
Annuity	Antiquated	Unappertizing	Application	Comprehensive
Approach	Approve	Appropriate	Art	Arbiter
Approachable	Approval	Appropriately	Artistry	Arbitrate
Approachability	Disapprove	Appropriateness	Artisan	Arbitration
Reproach	Disapproval	Inappropriate	Artifice	Arbitrator
Archaic	Rise	Rouse	Art	Appropriate
Archeology	Rising	Rousing	Artist	Appropriately
Archeologist	Riser	Arouse	Artistic	Misappropriate
Archeological	Arise	Arousal	Artistically	Misappropriation
Assess	Astound	Symmetry	Athlete	Type
Assessor	Astounding	Symmetrical	Athletic	Typical
Assessment	Astonish	Asymmetry	Athletics	Typically
Reassess	Astonishment	Asymmetrical	Athleticism	Atypical
Authentic	Automate	Avoid	Aware	Awake
Authenticity	Automation	Avoidable	Awareness	Awaken
Authenticate	Automatic	Avoidance	Beware	Wake
Authentication	Automatically	Unavoidable	Unaware	Wakeful
Baron	Bath	Calm	Behaviour	Witch
Baroness	Bathe	Calmly	Behave	Witchcraft
Baronet	Bather	Calmness	Misbehave	Bewitch
Baronial	Sunbathe	Becalmed	Misbehaviour	Bewitching
Monogamy	Blaspheme	Blood	Blow	BombBomber
Bigamy	Blasphemer	Bloody	Blowy	Bombard
Bigamist	Blasphemy	Blooded	Blower	Bombardment
Bigamous	Blasphemous	Bloodless	Blustery	.
.	.	.	.	.
.	.	.	.	.

Brother	Broad	Bulb	Bureau	Fan
Brotherly	Broadly	Bulbous	Bureaucracy	Fanatic
Brotherhood	Broaden	Bulge	Bureaucrat	Fanatical
Bretheren	Broadcast	Bulging	Bureaucratic	Fanaticism
Fancy	Fate	Father	Fertile	Fever
Fanciful	Fatalism	Fatherly	Fertility	Fevered
Fantasy	Fatalist	Fatherhood	Infertile	Feverish
Fantasize	Fatalistic	Fatherless	Infertility	Feverishly
Filth	Fit	Fizz	Flex	Fort
Filthy	Fitting	Fizzy	Flexible	Fortify
Filthily	Fitter	Fizziness	Flexibility	Fortification
Filthiness	Fitment	Fizzle	Inflexible	Fortress
Fraternal	Frequent	Frill	Frustrate	Fundamental
Fraternize	Frequently	Frilled	Frustration	Fundamentally
Fraternization	Frequency	Frilly	Frustrating	Fundamentalist
Fraternity	Infrequent	Fringe	Frustrated	Fundamentalism
Furnish	Fuss	Magic	Make	Mania
Furnishings	Fussy	Magical	Maker	Maniac
Furniture	Fussily	Magically	Making	Maniacal
Unfurnished	Fussiness	Magician	Remake	Manic
Manipulate	Marine	Master	Mean	Meditation
Manipulation	Mariner	Mastery	Meanly	Meditate
Manipulative	Maritime	Masterly	Meanness	Meditator
Manipulator	Marina	Masterful	Meanie	Meditative
Merit	Mind	Shape	Moist	Moment
Meritorious	Minder	Shapely	Moisten	Momentary
Meritocracy	Mindful	Shapeless	Moisture	Momentarily
Meretricious	Mindless	Misshapen	Moisturize	Momentous
Monocle	Monotone	Monster	Mourn	Myth
Monocular	Monotony	Monstrous	Mourning	Mythical
Binochular	Monotonous	Monstrously	Mourner	Mythology
Binochulars	Monotonously	Monstrosity	Mournful	Mythological
Minor	Race	Rapid	Rare	Claim
Minority	Racial	Rapidly	Rarely	Claimant
Major	Racism	Rapidity	Rarity	Reclaim
Majority	Racist	Rapids	Rarified	Reclamation
Recognize	Condition	Record	Recoup	Red
Recognition	Conditioner	Recorder	Recuperate	Redden
Recognizable	Recondition	Recording	Recuperation	Redness
Unrecognizable	Conditional	Prerecorded	Recuperative	Reddish

| . | . | . | . | . |
| . | . | . | . | . |

Reflect	Generate	Religion	Renounce	Repent
Reflection	Generation	Religious	Renunciation	Repentant
Reflective	Regenerate	Irreligious	Denounce	Repentance
Reflector	Regeneration	Religiously	Denunciation	Unrepentant
Report	Search	Reside	Resolute	Resonate
Reporter	Searching	Residence	Resolutely	Resonator
Unreported	Research	Resident	Resolution	Resonant
Reportedly	Researcher	Residential	Resolved	Resonance
Respire	Restore	Retrieve	View	Revive
Respiration	Restorer	Retrieval	Viewer	Revival
Respiratory	Restoration	Irretrievable	Review	Revivalist
Respirator	Restorative	Retriever	Reviewer	Revivalism
Write	Rheumatism	Rhythm	Rite	Rotate
Writer	Rheumatic	Rhythmic	Ritual	Rotation
Writing	Rheumaticky	Rhythmical	Ritually	Rotary
Rewrite	Rheumatoid	Rhythmicially	Ritualistic	Rotor
Royal	Ruminate	Table	Tax	Teach
Royally	Rumination	Tabular	Taxation	Teacher
Royalty	Ruminative	Tabulate	Taxable	Teaching
Royalist	Ruminant	Tabulation	Untaxable	Unteachable
Telephone	Tempt	Tenable	Tender	Terminal
Telephony	Tempting	Untenable	Tenderly	Terminus
Telephonist	Temptation	Tenacity	Tenderness	Terminally
Telephonic	Temptress	Tenacious	Tenderize	Terminate
Tire	Total	Touch	Transparent	Tremor
Tired	Totally	Touched	Transparency	Tremulous
Tiring	Totality	Touching	Translucent	Tremble
Tiresome	Totalitarian	Untouched	Translucency	Trembling
Trap	Troop	Trick	Trivial	Democracy
Trapped	Trooper	Trickster	Triviality	Democratic
Trapper	Troupe	Trickery	Trivialize	Democratically
Trappings	Trouper	Tricky	Trivia	Democrat
Dank	Defy	Defect	Demon	Demote
Damp	Defiant	Defective	Demonic	Demotion
Dampen	Defiantly	Defector	Demonically	Promote
Dampness	Defiance	Defection	Demonism	Promotion
Dense	Dental	Deny	Deposit	Demonstrate
Densly	Dentist	Denial	Depositor	Demonstration
Density	Dentistry	Deniable	Depository	Demonstrative
Condense	Denture	Undeniable	Depot	Demonstrable
.	.	.	.	.
.	.	.	.	.

Deserve	Destiny	Detect	Determined	Deviate
Deserved	Destined	Detectable	Determinedly	Deviation
Deserving	Predestined	Detector	Determination	Deviance
Undeserving	Destination	Undetectable	Predetermined	Deviant
Dictate	Diet	Dignity	Dine	Direct
Dictator	Dieter	Dignified	Dining	Directly
Dictatorship	Dietary	Dignitary	Diner	Directness
Dictatorial	Dietician	Undignified	Dinner	Indirect
Agree	Discern	Comfort	Embark	Inclined
Agreement	Discernable	Comfortable	Embarkation	Inclination
Disagree	Discerning	Uncomfortable	Disembark	Disinclined
Disagreement	Discernment	Discomfort	Disembarkation	Disinclination
Associate	Persuade	Dither	Distress	Diverse
Association	Persuasion	Dithery	Distressing	Diversity
Dissociate	Persuasive	Dithering	Distressingly	Diversify
Dissociation	Dissuade	Ditherer	Distressed	Diversification
Dog	Dogma	Drop	Dry	Distinguish
Dogged	Dogmatic	Droplet	Drying	Distinguished
Doggedly	Dogmatically	Drip	Dryness	Distinguishable
Doggedness	Dogmatism	Dripping	Drought	Indistinguishable
Dull	Dust	Dynamic	Pacify	Paralyse
Dully	Dusty	Dynamically	Pacification	Paralysis
Dullness	Dustiness	Dynamism	Pacifist	Paraplegic
Dullard	Duster	Dynamics	Pacifism	Paralytic
Parent	Participate	Pay	Permanent	Permit
Parental	Participation	Payment	Permanently	Permissable
Parenting	Participator	Payable	Permanence	Permission
Parentage	Participant	Payee	Impermanence	Permissive
Perpetual	Philosophy	Phonetic	Picture	Phosphate
Perpetually	Philosopher	Phonetics	Pictorial	Phosphorus
Perpetuate	Philosophize	Phonetically	Picturesque	Phosphorescence
Perpetuation	Philosophical	Phonology	Picaresque	Phosphorescent
Pity	Plausible	Poem	Pole	Predict
Piteous	Plausibility	Poet	Polar	Prediction
Piteful	Implausible	Poetry	Polarize	Predictable
Pitiable	Implausibility	Poetic	Polarization	Unpredictable
Disposed	Prevail	Priest	Pride	Prince
Disposition	Prevailing	Priestly	Proud	Princely
Predisposed	Prevalence	Priestood	Proudly	Princess
Predisposition	Prevalent	Priestess	Shame	Principality

Logic List English: Meaningful Words - Volume 3

Profit	Prompt	Expel	Prophet	Psychosis
Profitable	Prompter	Expulsion	Prophetic	Psychotic
Profitability	Unprompted	Repel	Prophecy	Psychopath
Profiteer	Impromptu	Repulsion	Prophesy	Psychopathic
Prove	Publish	Pulse	Punish	Celebrate
Proven	Publisher	Pulsate	Punishment	Celebration
Disprove	Publication	Pulsation	Punative	Celebrated
Unproven	Unpublished	Pulsar	Punishing	Celebrity
Change	Cheek	Cheer	Class	Centralize
Changeling	Cheeky	Cheerful	Classify	Centralization
Exchange	Cheekily	Cherily	Classifiable	Decentralize
Exchangeable	Cheekiness	Cheerless	Classification	Decentralization
Cleric	Cloth	Cleave	Coast	Collaborate
Clerical	Clothe	Cleaver	Coastal	Collaboration
Clergy	Clothing	Cloven	Coastline	Collaborative
Clergical	Clothes	Cleft	Coaster	Collaborator
Coarse	Cocky	Coincide	Command	Combat
Coarsely	Cockily	Coincidence	Commander	Combatant
Coarsen	Cockiness	Coincidental	Commandant	Combative
Coarseness	Cocksure	Coincidentally	Commandment	Non-combatant
Common	Commune	Company	Compete	Conform
Commonly	Communal	Companion	Competition	Conformity
Commoner	Communally	Companionship	Competitive	Conformist
Uncommon	Community	Companionable	Competitor	Non-conformist
Concern	Confess	Confuse	Genial	Conquer
Concerned	Confession	Confusion	Geniality	Conqueror
Unconcerned	Confessional	Confound	Congenial	Conquest
Concerning	Confessor	Confounded	Congeniality	Unconquerable
Consist	Conspire	Consume	Contend	Conceive
Consistency	Conspiracy	Consumer	Contender	Conception
Consistent	Conspirator	Consumption	Contention	Contraceptive
Consistently	Conspiratorial	Consumptive	Contentious	Contraception
Contrary	Contribute	Converge	Convert	Cooperate
Contrarily	Contribution	Convergence	Conversion	Cooperative
Contrariness	Contributor	Diverge	Converter	Cooperation
Contrariwise	Contributory	Divergence	Convertible	Uncooperative
Cook	Crown	Coordinate	Correspond	Vital
Cookery	Coronet	Coordination	Corresponding	Vitally
Cooker	Coronation	Coordinator	Correspondence	Vitality
Uncooked	Uncrowned	Uncoordinated	Correspondent	Vitals
.	.	.	.	.
.	.	.	.	.

Cost	Cosy	Coward	Craft	Crass
Costly	Cosily	Cowardly	Craftsman	Crassly
Costliness	Cosiness	Cowardice	Craftsmanship	Crassness
Cremate	Crack	Crisp	Crude	Cruel
Cremation	Crevice	Crisply	Crudely	Cruelly
Crematorium	Crevasse	Crispiness	Crudity	Cruelty
Crumb	Crystal	Culprit	Custody	Cute
Crumble	Crystalize	Culpable	Custodial	Cutely
Crumbly	Crystalization	Culpability	Custodian	Cuteness
Sample	Saliva	Saturate	Sauce	Savage
Sampling	Salivary	Saturation	Saucy	Savagery
Sampler	Salivate	Unsaturated	Saucily	Savagely
Scarce	Scandal	Seclude	Secretary	Schizoid
Scarcely	Scandalize	Secluded	Secretarial	Schizophrenia
Scarcity	Scandalous	Seclusion	Secretariat	Schizophrenic
Secrete	Sedate	Seed	Seem	Senate
Secretion	Sedation	Seedling	Seeming	Senator
Secretory	Sedative	Seedy	Seemingly	Senatorial
Senior	Serene	Series	Serious	Settle
Seniority	Serenely	Serial	Seriously	Settler
Junior	Serenity	Serialize	Seriousness	Settlement
Severe	Sewage	Shabby	Shake	Shape
Severely	Sewer	Shabbily	Shaky	Shapely
Severity	Sewerage	Shabbiness	Shakily	Shapeless
Shave	Shelf	Shock	Shine	Ship
Shaver	Shelving	Shocking	Shiny	Shipping
Shavings	Shelve	Shocker	Shiner	Shipment
Short	Shrill	Show	Silk	Sin
Shorten	Shrilly	Showy	Silky	Sinful
Shortage	Shrillness	Showily	Silken	Sinner
Simulate	Sister	Site	Skin	Slip
Simulator	Sisterly	Situate	Skinless	Slippery
Simulation	Sisterhood	Situation	Skinny	Slipper
Slug	Snap	Sneak	Solemn	Solicitor
Sluggish	Snappy	Sneaky	Solemnly	Solicitous
Sluggard	Snapper	Sneaking	Solemnity	Solicitude
Solitary	Sophist	Sour	Sparse	Spasm
Solitude	Sophistry	Sourly	Sparsely	Spasmodic
Solitaire	Sophism	Sourness	Sparseness	Spasmodically
.	.	.	.	.
.	.	.	.	.
.	.	.	.	.

Space	Speed	Spine	Sponge	Spontaneous
Spacious	Speedy	Spinal	Spongy	Spontaneously
Spatial	Speedily	Spineless	Sponger	Spontaneity
Stagnate	Standard	Star	Start	State
Stagnant	Standardize	Starry	Starter	Statement
Stagnation	Standardization	Stardom	Startle	Stately
Statue	State	Steep	Stern	Stick
Statuette	Status	Steeply	Sternly	Sticky
Statesque	Stature	Steepness	Sternness	Sticker
Stock	Stone	Strain	Streak	Stretch
Stockist	Stony	Strained	Streaky	Stretchy
Stocky	Stoned	Strainer	Streaker	Stretcher
Strike	String	Strip	Stuff	Stubborn
Striker	Stringed	Stripe	Stuffing	Stubbornly
Striking	Stringy	Stripy	Stuffy	Stubbornness
Strong	Suave	Continent	Sublime	Submit
Strongly	Suavely	Continental	Sublimate	Submission
Stronghold	Suavity	Subcontinent	Sublimation	Submissive
Subscribe	Suburb	Subtle	Subvert	Suck
Subscriber	Surburban	Subtly	Subversion	Suckle
Subscription	Suburbia	Subtlety	Subversive	Suckling
Suck	Sudden	Sultan	Super	Sumptuous
Suction	Suddenly	Sultana	Superb	Sumptuously
Sucker	Suddenness	Sultanate	Superbly	Sumptuousness
Summary	Supple	Supply	Sure	Superficial
Summarize	Supply	Supplies	Surely	Superficially
Summation	Suppleness	Supplier	Unsure	Superficiality
Surf	Suspend	Sweat	Swell	Surmount
Surfing	Suspense	Sweaty	Swelling	Surmountable
Surfer	Suspension	Sweater	Swollen	Insurmountable
Swift	Swim	Sycophant	Symptom	Synchronize
Swiftly	Swimming	Sycophantic	Symptomatic	Synchronization
Swiftness	Swimmingly	Sycophancy	Syndrome	Synchronous
Polite	Quantity	Query	Valiant	Essence
Impolite	Quantify	Question	Valour	Essential
Impolitely	Quantifiable	Questionable	Valorous	Quintessence
Velvet	Vein	Verb	Vent	Victor
Velveteen	Venous	Verbose	Ventilator	Victorious
Velour	Ventricle	Verbiage	Ventilation	Victory
.	.	.	.	.
.	.	.	.	.
.	.	.	.	.

Vitreous	Nitrogen	Vivid	Vulgar	Warm
Vitrify	Nitrous	Vivacious	Vulgarity	Warmth
Vitrification	Nitrate	Vivacity	Vulgarly	Warmly
Watch	Weed	Well	Whale	Whine
Watcher	Weeds	Unwell	Whaler	Whining
Watchable	Weedy	Welfare	Whaling	Whinger
Whistle	Who	Wicked	Wary	Eager
Whistler	Whom	Wickedly	Wariness	Eagerly
Whistling	Whose	Wickedness	Warily	Eagerness
Ecology	Win	Wing	Wool	Worse
Ecologist	Winner	Winged	Woolly	Worsen
Ecological	Winnings	Winger	Wollen	Worst
Wrap	Weave	Wreck	Nasty	Neutral
Wrapper	Weaver	Wrecker	Nastily	Neutrality
Wrapping	Woven	Wreckage	Nastiness	Neutralize
Nip	Nurse	Notorious	Novel	Controversy
Nippy	Nursery	Notoriously	Novelist	Controversial
Nipper	Nurture	Notoriety	Novelette	Incontrovertible
Novel	Obstinate	Oblique	Odd	Obtrude
Novelty	Obstinacy	Obliquely	Oddity	Obtrusive
Novice	Obdurate	Obliqueness	Oddments	Unobtrusive
Occasion	Occlude	Opinion	Orphan	Oscillate
Occasional	Occlusion	Opinionated	Orphanage	Oscillation
Occasionally	Occult	Opine	Orphaned	Oscillator
Osseous	Our	Element	Eloquent	Embryo
Ossify	Ours	Elemental	Eloquently	Embryology
Ossification	Ourselves	Elementary	Eloquence	Embryonic
Endemic	Roll	Thrall	Entire	Trench
Epidemic	Enrol	Thraldom	Entirely	Entrench
Pandemic	Enrollment	Enthral	Entirety	Entrenchment
Equivocal	Escalate	Espy	Eternal	Euphemism
Equivocate	Escalation	Espionage	Eternally	Euphemistic
Equivocation	De-escalate	Spy	Eternity	Euphemistically
Evacuate	Evade	Excavate	Excess	Exaggerate
Evacuation	Evasion	Excavation	Excessive	Exaggeratedly
Evacuee	Evasive	Excavator	Excessively	Exaggeration
Excuse	Example	Exploit	Opponent	Extort
Excusable	Exemplary	Exploitation	Exponent	Extortion
Inexcusable	Exemplify	Exploiter	Exponential	Extortionate
.	.	.	.	.
.	.	.	.	.
.	.	.	.	.

Gallant	Extravagant	Gang	Garden	Geriatric
Gallantly	Extravagance	Gangster	Gardener	Geriatrics
Gallantry	Extravaganza	Gangland	Gardening	Gerontology
Generous	Gas	Gather	Gaudy	Glamour
Generously	Gaseous	Gathering	Gaudiness	Glamorous
Generosity	Gassy	Gathers	Garish	Glamorize
Germ	Germinate	Glare	Glide	Gesture
Germicide	Germination	Glaring	Gliding	Gesticulate
Germicidal	Gestation	Glaringly	Glider	Gesticulation
Gloss	Glue	Grasp	Grate	Gratis
Glossy	Gluey	Grapple	Grater	Gratuity
Glossiness	Glutinous	Grasping	Grating	Gratuitous
Grey	Grim	Grime	Grip	Ground
Greyish	Grimly	Grimy	Gripping	Grounding
Greyness	Grimness	Griminess	Gripe	Groundless
Grit	Grub	Guise	Hair	Guarantee
Gritty	Grubby	Disguise	Hairy	Guaranteed
Grittiness	Grubbiness	Undisguised	Hairiness	Guarantor
Happy	Harass	Harsh	Hate	Haul
Happily	Harrassment	Harshly	Hatred	Haulage
Happiness	Harangue	Harshness	Hateful	Haulier
Hear	Heresy	Hoard	Hunt	Horizon
Hearing	Heretic	Hoarder	Hunter	Horizontal
Hearer	Heretical	Horde	Huntress	Horizontally
Humour	Hunger	Humiliate	Hyphen	Icon
Humorous	Hungry	Humiliation	Hyphenated	Iconoclast
Humorist	Hungrily	Humiliating	Hyphenation	Iconoclastic
Hypocrisy	Hysteria	Ignite	Balance	Ignominy
Hypocrite	Hysterical	Ignition	Imbalance	Ignominious
Hypocritical	Hysterics	Igneous	Unbalanced	Ignominiously
Illustrate	Immediate	Peril	Perturb	Impetuous
Illustration	Immediately	Perilous	Perturbation	Impetuosly
Illustrator	Immediacy	Imperil	Imperturbable	Impetuosity
Prompt	Irate	Irony	Respective	Reproach
Promptly	Irascible	Ironic	Respectively	Reproachful
Promptness	Irascibility	Ironically	Irrespective	Irreproachable
Inaugerate	Incinerate	Compatible	Competent	Incubate
Inaugeration	Incineration	Compatibility	Competence	Incubation
Inaugeral	Incinerator	Incompatible	Incompetence	Incubator
.	.	.	.	.
.	.	.	.	.
.	.	.	.	.

Indulge	Inebriate	Eligible	Inert	Inevitable
Indulgent	Inebriated	Eligibility	Inertia	Inevitably
Indulgence	Inebriation	Ineligible	Inertial	Inevitability
Expert	Extricate	Furnace	Infiltrate	Fight
Expertise	Extrication	Inferno	Infiltration	Fighter
Inexpert	Inextricable	Infernal	Infiltrator	Infighting
Fluid	Genius	Ingenue	Injure	Salutary
Fluidity	Ingenious	Ingenuous	Injury	Salubrious
Fluvial	Ingeniously	Ingenuously	Injurious	Insalubrious
Sanitary	Insect	Semen	Sinuous	Insolent
Sanitation	Insecticide	Inseminate	Insinuate	Insolently
Insanitary	Insectivorous	Insemination	Insinuation	Insolence
Instant	Instigate	Instinct	Insulate	Subordinate
Instantly	Instigation	Instinctive	Insulator	Insubordinate
Instantaneous	Instigator	Instinctively	Insulation	Insubordination
Insurrection	Intermittent	Intern	Disperse	Intimate
Insurgent	Intermittently	Internee	Dispersal	Intimately
Insurgency	Intermission	Internment	Interspersed	Intimacy
Invade	Invest	Involve	Labour	Invincible
Invader	Investor	Involved	Labourer	Invincibly
Invasion	Investment	Involvement	Laborious	Invincibility
Lament	Laugh	Launder	Lead	Letter
Lamentable	Laughter	Laundry	Leaded	Lettered
Lamentation	Laughable	Laundrette	Leaden	Lettering
Lingual	Loathe	Lose	Long	Juvenile
Linguist	Loathing	Loss	Longing	Rejuvenate
Linguistics	Loathsome	Loser	Longingly	Rejuvenation
Lubricate	Abrupt	Intricate	Abandon	Abbot
Lubrication	Abruptly	Intricately	Abandoned	Abbess
Lubricant	Abruptness	Intracacy	Abandonment	Abbey
Abhor	Bide	Abrade	Abstract	Abundant
Abhorrent	Abiding	Abrasion	Abstraction	Abundantly
Abhorrence	Abide	Abrasive	Abstracted	Abundance
Absurd	Abyss	Account	Academy	Accomodate
Absurdly	Abysmal	Recount	Academic	Accomodating
Absurdity	Abysmally	Discount	Academically	Accomodation
Curse	Achieve	Acoustic	Acrid	Acrobat
Cursed	Achievement	Acoustics	Acrimony	Acrobatic
Accursed	Achievable	Acoustically	Acrimonious	Acrobatics
.	.	.	.	.
.	.	.	.	.
.	.	.	.	.

Cross	Adapt	Adapt	Adhere	Adhere
Crossly	Adaptable	Adaptor	Adherence	Adhesion
Crossness	Adaptability	Adaption	Adherent	Adhesive
Adjoin	Adopt	Verb	Adverse	Aggrevate
Adjoining	Adoption	Adverb	Adversity	Aggrevation
Adjacent	Adoptive	Adverbial	Adversary	Aggrevating
Float	Agent	Agitate	Glow	Alter
Floating	Agency	Agitation	Glowing	Alteration
Afloat	Reagent	Agitator	Aglow	Unalterable
Agony	Ail	Aim	Alarm	Alcohol
Agonize	Ailing	Aimless	Alarming	Alcoholic
Agonizing	Ailment	Aimlessly	Alarmist	Alcoholism
Light	Allergy	Lure	Most	Alphabet
Alight	Allergen	Allure	Mostly	Alphabetical
Lighter	Allergic	Alluring	Almost	Alphabetically
Amalgam	Amuse	Ancestor	Angel	Anatomy
Amalgamate	Amusing	Ancestral	Angelic	Anatomical
Amalgamation	Amusement	Ancestry	Archangel	Anatomically
Anger	Angle	Nullify	Anonymity	Climax
Angry	Angler	Annul	Anonymous	Climactic
Angrily	Angling	Annulment	Anonymously	Anticlimax
Anxiety	Apology	Appeal	Appreciate	Architect
Anxious	Apologize	Appealing	Appreciative	Architecture
Anxiously	Apologetic	Appellant	Appreciation	Architectural
Arch	Aristocrat	Artful	Assassin	Artificial
Archly	Aristocracy	Artless	Assassinate	Artificially
Archness	Aristocratic	Artlessly	Assassination	Artificiality
Assert	Assist	Astrology	Atrocity	Attention
Assertion	Assistant	Astrologer	Atrocious	Attentive
Assertive	Assistance	Astrological	Atrociously	Attentiveness
Attain	Author	Audacity	Autocracy	Available
Attainable	Authoress	Audacious	Autocrat	Availability
Attainment	Authorship	Audaciously	Autocratic	Unavailable
Awe	Back	Bald	Bake	Awkward
Awesome	Backer	Balding	Baker	Awkwardly
Awful	Backing	Baldness	Bakery	Awkwardness
Baptism	Become	Beg	Bend	Bewilder
Baptist	Becoming	Beggar	Bent	Bewildering
Baptize	Unbecoming	Beggarly	Bendy	Bewilderment
.	.	.	.	.
.	.	.	.	.
.	.	.	.	.

Troth	Beast	Begin	Bigotry	Bitch
Betrothed	Bestial	Beginning	Bigot	Bitchy
Betrothal	Bestiality	Beginner	Bigoted	Bitchiness
Bind	Black	Bless	Block	Board
Binding	Blackness	Blessing	Blockage	Boarding
Binder	Blacken	Blessed	Blockade	Boarder
Blot	Bowl	Booze	Box	Brains
Blotch	Bowls	Boozy	Boxer	Brainy
Blotchy	Bowling	Boozer	Boxing	Brainless
Brave	Brash	Brew	Bumble	Buoy
Bravery	Brazen	Brewer	Bumbling	Buoyant
Bravado	Brazenly	Brewery	Bumbler	Buoyancy
Bungle	Burgle	Face	Facile	Fabled
Bungler	Burglary	Facial	Facility	Fabulous
Bungling	Burglar	Faceless	Facilitate	Fabulously
Fail	Farce	Fascinate	Fashion	Fathom
Failure	Farcical	Fascinating	Fashionable	Fathomable
Failing	Farcically	Fascination	Fashionably	Unfathomable
Fat	Fatal	Feasible	Feather	Fertilize
Fatty	Fatally	Feasibly	Feathered	Fertilizer
Fatten	Fatality	Feasibility	Feathery	Fertilization
Fence	Festive	Fibre	Fiddle	Fiend
Fencer	Festivity	Fibrous	Fidget	Fiendish
Fencing	Festival	Fibroid	Fidgety	Fiendishly
Fill	Fine	Firm	Fit	Flavour
Filling	Finely	Firmly	Fitting	Flavouring
Filler	Fineness	Firmness	Fitness	Flavourless
Flatter	Flaw	Fold	Flippant	Flirt
Flattery	Flawed	Folder	Flippantly	Flirtation
Flatterer	Flawless	Folio	Flippancy	Flirtatious
Flower	Follow	Forge	Formula	Fornicate
Floral	Following	Forger	Formulate	Fornication
Florist	Follower	Forgery	Formulation	Fornicator
Fossil	Found	Frank	Fragile	Fracture
Fossilize	Founder	Frankly	Fragility	Fragment
Fossilization	Foundation	Frankness	Frail	Fragmentation
Free	Fraction	Frisk	Frivolous	Function
Freeing	Fractional	Frisky	Frivolously	Functional
Freedom	Fractionally	Friskily	Frivolity	Dysfunctional
.	.	.	.	.
.	.	.	.	.
.	.	.	.	.

Frugal	Fun	Fumes	Fungus	Further
Frugally	Funny	Fumigate	Fungal	Furthest
Frugality	Funnily	Fumigation	Fungicide	Furthermore
Fur	Fury	Fuse	Machine	Magnanimous
Furry	Furious	Fusible	Machinery	Magnanimously
Furrier	Furiously	Fussion	Machinist	Magnamity
Treat	Margin	Mason	Magnify	Magnificent
Treatment	Marginal	Masonry	Magnification	Magnificently
Maltreat	Marginally	Masonic	Magnitude	Magnificence
Majesty	Practice	Medal	Meddle	Melancholy
Majestic	Practitioner	Medalist	Meddler	Melancholic
Majestically	Malpractice	Medallion	Meddlesome	Melancholia
Mediate	Meek	Mind	Merry	Merchant
Mediator	Meekly	Mental	Merrily	Merchandise
Mediation	Meekness	Mentally	Merriment	Mercantile
Mess	Metaphor	Meteor	Physical	Meteorology
Messy	Metaphorical	Meteorite	Metaphysics	Meteorologist
Messily	Metaphorically	Meteoric	Metaphysical	Meteorological
Mild	Million	Miracle	Mischief	Represent
Mildly	Millionth	Miraculous	Mischievous	Representative
Mildness	Millionaire	Miraculously	Mischievously	Misrepresent
Miser	Print	Mist	Monarch	Molest
Miserly	Printer	Misty	Monarchy	Molester
Miserable	Misprint	Mistiness	Monarchist	Molestation
Motive	Mood	Mug	Mutiny	Murder
Motivation	Moody	Mugger	Mutineer	Murderer
Motivate	Moodiness	Mugging	Mutinous	Murderous
Musket	Radical	Recite	Reckon	Reckless
Musketry	Radically	Recital	Reckoner	Recklessly
Musketeer	Radicalism	Recitation	Reckoning	Recklessness
Compensate	Double	Refer	Rectify	Reform
Compensation	Doubly	Referal	Rectification	Reformer
Recompense	Redouble	Reference	Rectifier	Reformation
Regard	Register	Regret	House	Regiment
Regardless	Registration	Regretful	Housing	Regimental
Regarding	Registry	Regrettable	Rehouse	Regimentation
Reluctant	Remain	Remark	Represent	Reminisce
Reluctantly	Remains	Remarkable	Representation	Reminiscence
Reluctance	Remainder	Remarkably	Representative	Reminiscent
.	.	.	.	.
.	.	.	.	.
.	.	.	.	.

Republic	Resent	Reserve	Retain	Retaliate
Republican	Resentment	Reservation	Retention	Retaliation
Republicanism	Resentful	Reserved	Retentive	Retaliatory
Retard	Retire	Retract	Retrograde	Return
Retarded	Retirement	Retraction	Retrogressive	Returnable
Retardation	Retiring	Retractable	Retrogression	Non-returnable
Union	Rigid	Rise	Risk	Rhetoric
Unionist	Rigidly	Rising	Risky	Rhetorical
Unionization	Rigidity	Uprising	Riskily	Rhetorically
Robot	Rock	Robust	Rock	Tantalize
Robotic	Rocky	Robustly	Rocky	Tantalizing
Robotics	Rocker	Robustness	Rockery	Tantalizingly
Rude	Rubber	Ruin	Rule	Ruthless
Rudiments	Rubbery	Ruinous	Ruler	Ruthlessly
Rudimentary	Rubberize	Ruination	Ruling	Ruthlessness
Run	Run	Talk	Tame	Telepathy
Running	Runny	Talkative	Tamely	Telepathic
Runner	Running	Talker	Tamer	Telepathically
Tactile	Teens	Tedious	Ten	Theatre
Tangible	Teenage	Tediously	Tenth	Theatrical
Tangibly	Teenager	Tedium	Tenner	Theatricals
Tense	Testate	Test	Thief	Thermostat
Tension	Testament	Testy	Thieve	Thermostatic
Tensile	Intestate	Testiness	Thieving	Thermostatically
Theology	Therapy	Thresh	Thug	Thorough
Theological	Therapist	Thrash	Thuggish	Thoroughly
Theologian	Therapeutic	Thrashing	Thuggery	Thoroughness
Thrill	Thrift	Thunder	Tile	Titillate
Thrilling	Thrifty	Thundery	Tiled	Titillation
Thriller	Thriftiness	Thunderous	Tiling	Titillating
Tin	Title	Top	Tough	Tonsil
Tinned	Titled	Topping	Toughen	Tonsillitis
Tinny	Titular	Topped	Toughness	Tonsillectomy
Topic	Tourism	Trade	Tragedy	Tradition
Topically	Tourist	Trader	Tragic	Traditional
Topicality	Touristy	Trading	Tragically	Traditionally
Transfer	Transform	Transgress	Translate	Transcend
Transferrable	Transformation	Transgression	Translation	Transcendence
Transferrance	Transformer	Transgressor	Translator	Transcendental
.	.	.	.	.
.	.	.	.	.
.	.	.	.	.

Transmit	Trauma	Travel	Treasure	Plant
Transmitter	Traumatize	Traveller	Treasury	Transplant
Transmission	Traumatic	Travelogue	Treasurer	Transplantation
Trend	Tribe	Triple	Trouble	Transport
Trendy	Tribal	Triplicate	Troubled	Transporter
Trendiness	Tribalism	Triplets	Troublesome	Transportation
Triumph	Trust	Tube	Daunt	Dazzle
Triumphal	Trustee	Tubing	Daunting	Dazzling
Triumphant	Trusteeship	Tubular	Dauntless	Dazzlingly
Deaf	Deal	Brief	Decorum	Decimal
Deafen	Dealings	Debrief	Decorous	Decimalize
Deafness	Dealer	Debriefing	Indecorous	Decimalization
Dedicate	Defer	Defer	Deficit	Function
Dedicated	Deferral	Deference	Deficient	Functional
Dedication	Deferment	Deferential	Deficiency	Defunct
Flat	Deflect	Defoliate	Deft	Degenerate
Flatten	Deflection	Defoliation	Deftly	Degeneration
Flatness	Deflector	Defoliate	Deftness	Degeneracy
Fraud	Deity	Dejected	Demented	Deliver
Fraudulent	Deify	Dejectedly	Dementedy	Delivery
Defraud	Deification	Dejection	Dementia	Deliverance
Delirium	Demolish	Depart	Depute	Morale
Delirious	Demolisher	Departure	Deputize	Demoralize
Deliriously	Demolition	Departed	Deputy	Demoralization
Deprecate	Appreciate	Derive	Descend	Dermatitis
Deprecation	Depreciate	Derivative	Descended	Dermatology
Deprecatory	Depreciation	Derivation	Descendant	Dermatologist
Desert	Despise	Despot	Detect	Detest
Deserter	Despicable	Despotically	Detective	Detestable
Desertion	Despicably	Despotism	Detection	Detestation
Throne	Detonate	Devastate	Devious	Agreeable
Enthrone	Detonation	Devastated	Deviously	Disagreeable
Dethrone	Detonator	Devastation	Deviousness	Disagreeably
Dirt	Devote	Diagnose	Diction	Digress
Dirty	Devoted	Diagnosis	Dictate	Digression
Dirtiness	Devotedly	Diagnostic	Dictation	Digressive
Digit	Diligent	Diplomacy	Bursar	Disaster
Digital	Diligently	Diplomat	Bursary	Disasterous
Digitally	Diligence	Diplomatic	Disburse	Disasterously
.	.	.	.	.
.	.	.	.	.
.	.	.	.	.

Discipline	Inter	Prove	Dissent	Recover
Disciplinary	Inerment	Proven	Dissenter	Recovery
Disciplinarian	Disinter	Disprove	Dissention	Recoverable
Distribute	Divine	Dizzy	Docile	Divert
Distribution	Divenly	Dizzily	Docilely	Diversion
Distributor	Divinity	Dizziness	Docility	Diversionary
Doctor	Dodder	Domicile	Donate	Document
Doctoral	Doddery	Domicillary	Donation	Documentation
Doctorate	Dodderer	Domestic	Donor	Documentary
Dowdy	Draper	Draught	Dream	Dreary
Dowdily	Drapery	Draughty	Dreamer	Drearily
Dowdiness	Drapes	Draughtiness	Dreamy	Dreariness
Dregs	Drizzle	Duel	Paint	Duration
Dredge	Drizzly	Duelling	Painer	Durable
Dredger	Drench	Duellist	Painting	Durability
Dwell	Pale	Panel	Palate	Paradox
Dwelling	Palings	Panelling	Palatable	Paradoxical
Dweller	Palisade	Panellist	Unpalatable	Paradoxically
Pardon	Parley	Pedant	Pension	Pathology
Pardonable	Parliament	Pedantic	Pensioner	Pathologist
Unpardonable	Parliamentary	Pedantry	Pensionable	Pathological
Period	Perish	Perform	Permeate	Perpetrate
Periodic	Perishable	Performer	Permeable	Perpetrating
Periodically	Perishing	Performance	Impermeable	Perpetrator
Persecute	Pirate	Plain	Plan	Philanthropy
Persecution	Piracy	Plainly	Planning	Philanthropic
Persecutor	Piratical	Plainess	Unplanned	Philanthropist
Plenty	Plod	Pluck	Plumb	Predominant
Plentiful	Plodder	Plucky	Plumber	Predominance
Plentious	Plodding	Pluckily	Plumbing	Predominate
Plunge	Point	Poison	Pollute	Porter
Plunger	Pointed	Poisoner	Pollution	Portable
Plunging	Pointedly	Poisonous	Pollutant	Portability
Pose	Portray	Post	Pothole	Occupied
Poser	Portait	Postal	Potholer	Preoccupied
Posing	Portrayal	Postage	Potholing	Preoccupation
Powder	Pretty	President	Prescribe	Procrastinate
Powdered	Prettily	Presidency	Prescription	Procrastination
Powdery	Prettiness	Presidential	Prescriptive	Procrastinator
.	.	.	.	.
.	.	.	.	.
.	.	.	.	.

Logic List English: Meaningful Words - Volume 3

Procure	Process	Projector	Prolific	Program
Procurer	Procedure	Projection	Proliferate	Programmer
Procurement	Proceedings	Projectionist	Proliferation	Programmable
Provide	Prominent	Propel	Prosper	Protract
Provider	Prominently	Propulsion	Prosperous	Protraction
Provision	Prominence	Propellant	Prosperity	Protractive
Proviso	Providence	Provoke	Prude	Prudent
Provision	Providential	Provocation	Prudery	Prudence
Provisional	Provident	Provocative	Prudish	Prudential
Psyche	Province	Publicize	Puppet	Puzzle
Psychic	Provincial	Publicity	Puppetry	Puzzling
Psychical	Provincialism	Publicist	Puppeteer	Puzzlement
Push	Pursue	Canon	Cannibal	Calcium
Pushy	Pursuer	Canonize	Cannibalism	Calcify
Pusher	Pursuit	Canonization	Cannibalize	Calcification
Candid	Can	Captive	Cardiac	Caustic
Candidly	Canned	Captivation	Cardiology	Cauterize
Candour	Cannery	Captivating	Cardiologist	Cauterization
Catalyst	Challenge	Chance	Chapel	Ceremony
Catalyse	Challenger	Chancer	Chaplain	Ceremonial
Catalytic	Unchallenged	Chancy	Chaplaincy	Ceremoniously
Charity	Chasten	Chauvenism	Chief	Cinema
Charitable	Chastise	Chauvenist	Chieftain	Cinematography
Uncharitable	Chastisement	Chauvenistic	Chiefly	Cinematographer
Child	Chlorine	Civility	Clarity	Classic
Childish	Chlorinate	Civilize	Clarify	Classical
Childishly	Chlorination	Civilization	Clarification	Classically
Clear	Clear	Clever	Clip	Coagulate
Clearance	Clearly	Cleverly	Clippiers	Coagulation
Clearing	Clearness	Cleverness	Clipping	Coagulant
Close	Cloud	Clumsy	Code	Commentate
Closely	Cloudy	Clumsily	Codify	Commentator
Closeness	Cloudless	Clumsiness	Codification	Commentary
Coerce	Cold	Misery	Compact	Member
Coercion	Coldly	Commiserate	Compactly	Dismember
Coercive	Coldness	Commiseration	Compactness	Dismemberment
Compile	Compose	Complain	Reveal	Commerce
Compiler	Composer	Complaint	Conceal	Commercial
Compilation	Composition	Complainant	Concealment	Commercialize
.	.	.	.	.
.	.	.	.	.
.	.	.	.	.

Depart	Concede	Current	Condense	Commence
Department	Concession	Currently	Condenser	Commencement
Departmental	Concessionary	Concurrently	Condensation	Recommence
Condemn	Confine	Confection	Cone	Congratulate
Condemnation	Confined	Confectioner	Conifer	Congratulation
Condemnatory	Confinement	Confectionery	Coniferous	Congratulatory
Congress	Console	Consul	Conspicuous	Conscience
Congressman	Consolation	Consular	Conspicuously	Conscientious
Congessational	Inconsolable	Consulate	Inconspicuous	Conscientiously
Contact	Contain	Contempt	Contest	Contemplate
Contagion	Containment	Contemptible	Contestant	Contemplation
Contagious	Container	Contemptuous	Uncontested	Contemplative
Contradict	Contrite	Contrive	Convene	Conventional
Contradiction	Contritely	Contrived	Convener	Conventially
Contradictory	Contrition	Contrivance	Convention	Unconventional
Convalesce	Obverse	Convince	Convulse	Correlate
Convalescent	Converse	Convincing	Convulsion	Correlation
Convalescence	Conversely	Conviction	Convulsive	Correlative
Cordial	Corrugate	Corroborate	.	.
Cordially	Corrugation	Corroboration	.	.
Cordiality	Corrugated	Corraborative	.	.

PART TWO

THE REAL WORLD

SECTION 1

THE PHYSICAL WORLD

Logic List English: Meaningful Words - Volume 3

UNIVERSE	PLANET	EARTH	LANDSCAPE	MINERALS
Space	Pluto	Air	Mountains	Rock
Galaxy	Saturn	Land	Volcanoes	Boulder
Solar System	Uranus	Water	Plateau	Stone
Star	Neptune	Continents	Peak	Pebble
Planet	Jupiter	Islands	Range	Granite
Sun	Mars	Ice sheets	Hill	Sandstone
Moon	Venus	Sea	Desert	Quartz
Asteroid	Mercury	Ocean	Grassland	Flint
Meteor	Earth	Lake	Scrub	Clay
.	Crater	Pond	Wood	Mud
.	Orbit	River	Forest	Sand
.	Atmosphere	Stream	Jungle	Dust

RANGES	PEAKS	WEATHER	OCEANS	SEAS
Pyrenees	Everest	Snow	Atlantic	South China
Alps	Fujiyama	Hail	Pacific	Caspian
Urals	Kilimanjaro	Ice	Indian	Black
Caucasus	Etna	Rain	Arctic	Coral
Cascades	Vesuvius	Storm	Antarctic	Mediterranean
Rockies	Eiger	Frost	.	Baltic
Andes	Matterhorn	Thunder	.	North Sea
Himalayas	Mt McKinley	Lightning	.	Irish Sea
Blue Mts	Snowden	Wind	.	English Channel
.	Ben Nevis	Mist	.	Suez Canal
.	.	Fog	.	Panama Canal
.	.	Cloud	.	.
.	.	Tornado	.	.
.	.	Hurricane	.	
.	.	Monsoon	.	

				AMERICA
				USA
LAKES	RIVERS	CONTINENTS	NATIONS	Canada
Loch Ness	Thames	Europe	Empires	Mexico
Windermere	Clyde	Asia	Kingdoms	Chile
Geneva	Danube	Africa	Countries	Argentina
Ontario	Rhine	North America	Cities	Uruguay
Superior	Volga	South America	Towns	Paraguay
Michigan	Seine	.	Villages	Brazil
Huron	Nile	.	Hamlets	Columbia
Erie	Amazon		.	Nicaragua
Dead sea*	Mississippi	*Really a lake	.	.

Logic List English: Meaningful Words - Volume 3

AFRICA	NEAR EAST	FAR EAST	EASTERN EUROPE	WESTERN EUROPE
Chad	Israel	China	Russia	Britain
Congo	Lebanon	Japan	Poland	England
Zambia	Turkey	Korea	Bulgaria	Ireland
Zimbabwe	Iran	Thailand	Rumania	Scotland
Namibia	Iraq	Burma	Albania	Wales
Kenya	Syria	Tibet	Hungary	Germany
Malawi	Libya	Mongolia	Yugoslavia	Austria
Madagascar	Egypt	Malaysia	Czechoslovakia	Switzerland
Somalia	Sudan	Singapore	Estonia	Sweden
Ethiopia	Morocco	Borneo	Latvia	Norway
Nigeria	Algeria	Sumatra	Lithuania	Finland
Gold Coast	Saudi Arabia	India	.	Iceland
Gambia	Yemen	Pakistan	.	Holland
South Africa	.	Afghanistan	.	Netherlands
Uganda	.	Australia	.	Belgium
Botswana	.	New Zealand	.	France
.	.			Spain
CITIES	UK TOWNS	COUNTIES	BUILDINGS	Portugal
New York	London	Powys	Office Block	Italy
Washington	Birmingham	Glamorgan	Factory	Greece
Berlin	Manchester	Kent	Hotel	
Paris	Bradford	Surrey	Hospital	.
Brussels	Newcastle	Devon	Care Home	SHOPS
Amsterdam	Glasgow	Dorset	Cathedral	Sports Shop
Geneva	Edinburgh	Cornwall*	Church	Ironmonger
Lisbon	Aberdeen	Home Counties	Chapel	Hardware Store
Madrid	Dundee	East Anglia	Police Station	Department Store
Rome	Cardiff	South West	Fire Station	Coffee Shop
Venice	Swansea	Midlands	Post Office	Paper Shop
Rio	Dublin	Lowlands	Bank	Stationers
Moscow	Cork	Highlands	.	Book Shop
Pekin	Norwich	Borders	.	Chemist
Seoul	Ipswich	Central Belt	.	Pharmacy
Shanghai	Dover	.	.	Butcher
Tokyo	Cambridge	.	.	Baker
New Delhi	Oxford	.	.	Grocer
Calcutta	.	* Most counties	.	Supermarket
Sydney	.	go under 'shire'	.	Hairdresser
Cape Town	.	and were covered	.	Barber shop
Lagos	.	in the last book	.	.
.	.		.	

ACCOMMO-DATION	PARTS OF BUILDING	HOUSE INTERIOR	ROOMS	LOUNGE CONTENTS
House	Roof	Paint	Attic	Couch
Flat	Walls	Whitewash	Loft	Sofa
Apartment	Floor	Door frame	Stairs	Settee
Penthouse	Windows	Skirting Board	Landing	Cupboard
Mansion	Doors	Door Knobs	Bedroom	Fireplace
Cottage	Bricks	Locks	Bathroom	Radiators
Farm House	Mortar	Hinge	En suite	Rug
Castle	Foundations	Catches	Toilet	Mat
Holiday Home	Tiles	Windowsills	Shower	Curtains
Hotel Room	Slates	Mantlepiece	Lounge	Blinds
Bed and Breakfast	Corrugated Iron	Sockets	Sitting Room	Table
Guest House	Chimney	Light Fitting	Dining Room	Chairs
Caravan	Plasterboard	.	Kitchen	Cushion
Tent	Asbestos	.	Cellar	Stool
.	Pipes	.	Basement	Vase
.	Electrical Cables	.	Garage	Lights
.	.	.	.	Mirror
.	.	.	.	.

BEDROOM	KITCHEN	UTENSILS	BATHROOM	ELECTRICAL GOODS
Pillow	Cooker	Knife	Bath	TV
Duvet	Microwave	Fork	Shower	Radio
Quilt	Oven	Spoon	Sink	Games Console
Blanket	Rings	Ladle	Hose	DVD Player
Sheet	Kettle	Whisk	Tap	Music Centre
Mattress	Washing Machine	Tea Strainer	Plug	Computer
Dressing Table	Dishwasher	Spatula	Scales	Laptop
Chest of drawers	Fridge	Bowl	Towel	Mobile Phone
Carpet	Freezer	Dish	Flannel	Telephone
Headboard	Grill	Plate	Soap	Remote Control
Base	Toaster	Potato Peeler	Shower Gel	Router
Electric Blanket	Food mixer	Tin Opener	Shampoo	Filter
Wardrobe	Percolator	Garlic Press	Razor	Battery
.	Cafetiere	Saucepan	Shaving Soap	Clock
.	.	Frying Pan	Toilet	Ariel
.	.	.	Cistern	Satellite Dish
.	.	.	.	Camera
.	.	.	.	Video Camera
.	.	.	.	Printer

SEWING	FEMALE ATTIRE	MEN'S CLOTHING	FOOTWEAR	PERSONAL POSSESSIONS
Scissors	Dress	Suit	Shoes	Wallet
Needle	Skirt	Jacket	Socks	Purse
Cotton	Blouse	Jumper	Stilettos	Handbag
Thread	Slacks	Cardigan	High Heels	Make Up Kit
Wool	Tights	Shirt	Laces	Compact
Pin	Stockings	Trousers	Velcro	Lipstick
Safety Pin	Shawl	Jeans	Boots	Mascara
Zip	Scarf	Shorts	Slippers	Watch
Button	Bra	T-Shirt	Sandals	Money
Seams	Underwear	Waistcoat	.	Notes
Pocket	Nightdress	Cuffs	.	Small Change
Knitting Needles	Coat	Collar	.	Cigarettes
Sewing Machine	Hat	Cap	.	Lighter
.	Gloves	Tie	.	Matches
.	Dressing Gown	Pyjamas	.	Cigar
				Pipe

TOOLS	ACCESSORIES	GARDEN TOOLS	FLOWERS	GARDEN
Hammer	Nails	Spade	Rose	Backyard
Mallet	Screws	Shovel	Honeysuckle	Fence
Saw	Bolts	Garden Fork	Clematis	Hedge
Hacksaw	Nuts	Broom	Dahlia	Gate
Screwdriver	Washers	Rake	Aster	Shed
Drill	Rawl Plugs	Hoe	Orchid	Flower Bed
Clamp	Fuse	Trowel	Begonia	Compost
Axe	Plug	Shears	Daisy	Plants
Chopper	Wire	Lawn Edger	Hyacinth	Bulbs
Bradawl	Dowling Rod	Secateurs	Iris	Seeds
Tape Measure	Light socket	Shears	Jasmine	Shrubs
Spirit Level	.	Hedge Trimmer	Tulip	Fruit Trees
Wire Cutters	.	Strimmer	Daffodil	Lawn
File	.	Mower	Narcissus	Patio
Chisel	.	Watering Can	Poppy	Gazebo
Spanner	.	Hose	Chrysanthemum	.
Pliers	.	Flower pot	Cactus	.
Punch	.	Galoshes	.	.
Pincers	.	Rubber boots	.	.
Brush	.	Bulbs	.	.
Dustpan	.	Seeds	.	.

Logic List English: Meaningful Words - Volume 3

VEGETABLES	FRUIT	WHEAT PRODUCTS	SNACKS	CONDIMENTS
Cabbage	Apple	Bread	Burger	Salad Dressing
Cauliflower	Pear	Rolls	Hot Dog	Gravy
Brussel Sprouts	Peach	Baps	Pork Pie	Mayonnaise
Celery	Plum	Cake	Cheese Roll	Horseradish
Cucumber	Orange	Biscuits	Bacon Sandwich	Mustard
Tomatoes	Mandarin	Tarts	Ham Sandwich	Chilli
Peppers	Lemon	Fruitcake	Kebab	Vinegar
Onions	Lime	Bun Donut	Pickled Egg	Pepper
Garlic	Pomegranate	Cup cake	Gherkin	Salt
Peas	Banana	Tea cake	Cheese on Toast	.
Beans	Pineapple	Chelsea Bun	Beans on Toast	.
Mushrooms	Fig	Scone	Yogurt	.
Potatoes	Dates	Muffin	Crisps	.
Squash	Grape	Crumpet	Peanuts	.
Pumpkin	Cherry	Pancake	Ploughman's	.
Marrow	.	Crust	Soup	.
Turnip	.	.	Stew	.
Swede	.	.	Pizza	.
Beetroot	.	.	Macaroni Cheese	.
Lettuce	.	.	_____	.
_____	.	.	.	.
.	.	.	DINNER	.
SPREADS	HERBS & SPICES	BREAKFAST	Roast Beef	DESSERT
Butter	Mace	Cereal	Lamb Cutlet	Rice Pudding
Margarine	Ginger	Corn Flakes	Pork Chops	Cheesecake
Jam	Peppermint	Muesli	Mashed Potatoes	Apple Pie
Marmalade	Thyme	Toast	Roast Potatoes	Tapioca Pudding
Honey	Rosemary	Omelette	Gammon Steak	Ice Cream
Marmite	Cardamom	Bacon Rashers	Mutton	Gateau
Lemon Curd	Sage	Hash Browns	Steak & Kidney	Chocolate Cake
Chocolate Spread	Cinnamon	Fried Tomatoes	Chicken Pie	Pavlova
Peanut Butter	Nutmeg	Fried Eggs	Liver & Onions	Flan
.	Basil	Baked Beans	Fish & Chips	Sponge Cake
.	Cumin	Sausages	Turkey	Stewed Prunes
.	Parsley	.	Stuffing	Custard
.	.	.	Curry	Blancmange
.	.	.	Salad	Jelly
.	.	.	Coleslaw	.
.	.	.	Potato Salad	.
.	.	.	Pasta	.
.	.	.	Spaghetti	.

SWEETS	DRINKS	ALCOHOL	MIXERS	FIREWORKS
Lollipop	Tea	Beer	Ginger Ale	Rocket
Toffee	Coffee	Wine	Ginger Beer	Catherine Wheel
Chew	Hot Chocolate	Spirit	Soda Water	Roman Candle
Chewing Gum	Horlicks	Whisky	Tonic water	Sparklers
Liquorice	Ovaltine	Stout	Lemonade	Bangers
Chocolate	Milk	Vodka	Coke	Squib
Mints	Milk Shake	Brandy	Glass	Gunpowder
Gob Stopper	Mineral Water	Rum	Tumbler	Fuse
Wine Gums	Soft Drink	Bacardi	.	.
Jelly Babies	Lemonade	Tequila	.	.
.	Cream	Sherry	.	.
.	Sugar	Port	.	.
.	Cup	Champagne	.	.
.	Saucer	Lager	.	.
.	Mug	Cocktail	.	.
.	Glass	Bottle	.	.

PASTIMES	ENTERTAIN-MENT	THEATRE & FILM	VARIETY ACTS	CIRCUS
Jigsaw	Films	Producer	Dancer	Acrobat
Ludo	Cinema	Director	Singer	Strong Man
Tiddlywinks	Picture House	Actor	Ventriloquist	Bearded Lady
Monopoly	Theatre	Actress	Novelty Act	Lion Tamer
Chess	Ballet	Stage Manager	Magician	Ring Master
Dominoes	Opera	Leading Lady	Conjuror	Trapeze Artist
Marbles	Music Hall	Leading Man	Chorus Girl	High Wire Act
Crosswords	Disco	Understudy	Comic	Juggler
Snakes & Ladders	Night Club	Stand-in	Comedian	Clown
Playing Cards	Casino	Stunt Man	Orchestra Pit	Big Top
Patience	Seats	Cameraman	Puppet	Sideshow
Snap	Box Office	Play	Microphone	Caged Animals
Dice	Auditorium	Drama	.	Sawdust
Counters	.	.	.	Whip
Board	.	.	.	.
Ten Pin Bowling	.	.	.	.
Bowls	.	.	.	.
Darts	.	.	.	.
Billiards	.	.	.	.
Snooker	.	.	.	.
Pool	.	.	.	.
Scrabble	.	.	.	.

ARTISTS & WRITERS	DANCE	MUSIC	STRINGS & KEYBOARD	WIND & PERCUSSION
Author	Tango	Tune	Organ	Drums
Playwright	Waltz	Song	Piano	Cymbals
Typewriter	Foxtrot	Symphony	Harpsichord	Bongoes
Word Processor	Jive	Conductor	Synthesizer	Tubular Bells
Painter	Twist	Soloist	Double Bass	Xylophone
Portrait	Flamenco	Group	Cello	Glockenspiel
Landscape	Paso Doble	Brass Band	Fiddle	Flute
Photographer	Rumba	String Quartet	Violin	Oboe
Picture	Samba	Blues	Guitar	Saxophone
Image	Salsa	Rock	Banjo	Trumpet
Camera	Cha-cha-cha	Pop	Ukelele	Trombone
Drawing	Charleston	Classical	Harp	Bugle
Watercolour	Latin	Jazz	.	Bassoon
Oil Painting	Ballroom	Folk	.	Clarinet
Abstract	Costumes	.	.	Accordion
Brush	.	.	.	Harmonica
Palette	.	.	.	Mouth Organ
Frame	.	.	.	.

EDUCATION	SCHOOL	SUBJECTS	GEOMETRY	TIME PERIODS
University	Pen	Arithmetic	Line	Day
College	Pencil	Mathematics	Triangle	Night
School	Ruler	English	Square	Evening
Lecturer	Rubber	Reading	Oblong	Afternoon
Professor	Desk	Writing	Cube	Morning
Teacher	Calculator	Languages	Orb	Easter
Headmaster	Set Square	Science	Circle	Whitsun
Student	Compass	Religion	Pyramid	Christmas
Pupil	Chalk	Sport	Ovoid	New Year
Classroom	Duster	Domestic Science	Circumference	Spring Break
Bunsen Burner	Board	Computing	Diameter	Summer Holiday
Test Tube	Uniform	Politics	.	Half Term
Flask	.	Philosophy	.	Football Season
Experiment	.	Biology	.	Fishing Season
.	.	Zoology	.	Birthday
.	.	Physics	.	Anniversary
.	.	Chemistry	.	Centenary

SCIENCE & TECHNOLOGY	SPACE	METALS	MATERIALS	SUBSTANCES
Nuclear Reactor	Rocket	Iron	Plastic	Bromide
Wind Turbine	Shuttle	Steel	Polythene	Fluoride
Power Station	Space Station	Mercury	Polystyrene	Chloride
Electricity	Astronaut	Lead	Bakelite	Sulphuric
Gas	Cosmonaut	Bronze	Glass	Hydrochloric
Coal	Satellite	Copper	Foam	Nicotine
Waterworks	Astronomy	Nickel	Wood	Alcohol
Sewage	Telescope	Gold	Paper	Bleach
Laser	Stars	Silver	Cardboard	Arsenic
Magnetism	Constellations	Platinum	Hardboard	Cyanide
Pylons	Colonisation	Aluminium	Plywood	Strychnine
Telegraph Poles	Mission	Titanium	Chipboard	Aconite
Radiation	Gravity	Chromium	.	Acid
Radio Signals	Weightlessness	Pewter	.	Alkali
Fusion	.	.	.	Poison
Fission	.	.	.	.
Engineer	.	.	.	.
Atom	ILLNESS & INJURY	.	.	.
Robotics	Cold	.	.	.

PHARMACY	Influenza	SYMPTOMS	HOSPITAL	TREATMENT
Pills	Mumps	Fever	Doctor	Scalpel
Tablets	Measles	Headache	Nurse	Stethoscope
Capsules	Diphtheria	Abscess	Midwife	Thermometer
Bandages	Pneumonia	Earache	Surgeon	Mask
Plasters	Salmonella	Cramp	Matron	Gown
Tincture	Ricketts	Runny Nose	Consultant	Forceps
Ointment	Typhoid	Cough	Registrar	Swab
Oil of Cloves	Malaria	Sneeze	Sister	Syringe
Syrup of Figs	Migraine	Sores	Porter	Oxygen Mask
Cod Liver Oil	Fracture	Spots	Registrar	Ward
Toothpaste	Break	Throbbing	Receptionist	Theatre
Toothbrush	Dislocation	Swelling	Ambulance	Trolley
Shaving Cream	Bruise	Pains	Stretcher	Hospital Bed
.	Graze	Paralysis	Birth	.
.	Sprain	Faint	Death	.
.	Torn Ligament	Collapse	Disease	.
.	Cut	Unconscious	.	.
.	Cancer	.	.	.
.	Diabetes	.	.	.
.	Heart Attack	.	.	.

BODY PARTS	LIMBS	JOINTS	FACE	BONES
Head	Arms	Shoulders	Eyes	Skull
Neck	Legs	Elbows	Ears	Spine
Chest	Hands	Wrists	Nose	Ribs
Stomach	Feet	Knuckles	Mouth	Pelvis
Back	Fingers	Hips	Chin	Shoulder Blades
Bottom	Toes	Knees	Cheeks	Shin Bones
Backside	Thighs	Ankles	Brow	Vertebra
Privates	Calves	.	Temples	Femur
Breasts	Forearms	.	Eye Lids	Radius
Belly Button	Upper Arms	.	Lashes	Ulna
Waist	.	.	Lips	Tibia
Privates	.	.	Tongue	Fibula
.	.	.	Gums	Knee Cap
.	.	.	Teeth	.
.	.	.	Hair	.
.	.	.	.	.

INTERNAL ORGANS	SIGHT	SOUND	TOUCH	TASTE & SMELL
Brain	See	Hear	Feel	Bitter
Heart	Light	Listen	Hard	Salty
Lungs	Dark	Talk	Soft	Sweet
Liver	Colours	Noise	Sharp	Sour
Kidney	Objects	Loudness	Blunt	Tart
Stomach	Movement	Quiet	Hot	Sharp
Bladder	Black	Harsh	Cold	Acrid
Intestines	White	Sharp	Warm	Stink
Muscles	Brown	Shrill	Rough	Odour
Tendons	Red	Snap	Smooth	Sweet
Tissue	Yellow	Crackle	Coarse	Perfumed
Skin	Green	Pop	Rough	Scented
Nerves	Blue	Bang	.	.
Arteries	Orange	.	.	.
Veins	Pink	.	.	.
Blood	Purple	.	.	.
Urine	.	.	.	.
Tears	.	.	.	.
Glands	.	.	.	.
Ligaments	.	.	.	.

BODY SIZE	EMOTIONS	ATTITUDES	MENTAL ILLNESS	MENTAL HEALTH
Fat	Joy	Faith	Stress	Psychologist
Thin	Hope	Envy	Depression	Psychiatrist
Short	Shout	Jealousy	PTSD	Psychoanalyst
Tall	Cry	Respect	Schizophrenia	Counsellor
Small	Weep	Indifference	Sociopath	Sociologist
Large	Fear	Like	Psychopath	Social Worker
Gigantic	Terror	Love	Megalomania	Health Visitor
Big	Grief	Hate	Paranoia	Therapist
Muscular	Laugh	Guilt	Mania	Care Assistant
Athletic	Scream	Loathing	Bipolar	.
Broad Chested	Despair	Horror	.	.
Shapely	Sadness	Blame	.	.
Wide Hipped	Anger	Gloat	.	.
Long Limbed	Laugh	Shame	.	.

RELIGION	CHURCH	SERVICES	GOVERNMENT	COUNCIL
Pope	Chapel	Fire Brigade	President	Mayor
Archbishop	Cathedral	Police	Prime Minister	Town Clerk
Cardinal	Vestry	Ambulance	Chancellor	Councillor
Bishop	Diocese	Sewage Works	Minister	Town Hall
Dean	Graveyard	Health Service	House of Lords	Dustman
Deacon	Gravestone	Power	MP	Dustcart
Chaplain	Cross	Transport	Chief Whip	Road Sweeper
Vicar	Coffin	Military	The Opposition	Housing Dept.
Rector	Gargoyle	Council	Conservative	Roads Dept.
Reverend	Stained Glass	*Local - government*	Labour	Sewage
Choir	Bible	.	Liberal	.
Saint	Mitre	.	Election	.
Registrar	Dog Collar	.	Chief Whip	.
Marriage	Robes	.	Speaker	.
Christening	Vestments	.	*House of - commons*	.
Funeral	Pew	.	*Leader of the - house*	.
Cremation	Pulpit	.	*Member of - parliament*	.
Burial	Hymn Book	.		.
.	Congregation	.		.
.	Funeral	.		.
.	Undertaker	.		.

THE LAW	COURTROOM	POLICE	VIOLENT CRIME	STEALING
Lord Chief	High Court	Chief Constable	Poison	Robbery
Justice	Courtroom	Commissioner	Shoot	Theft
Judge	Stand	Superintendent	Stab	Fraud
Solicitor	Bench	Inspector	Attack	Defraud
Lawyer	Wig	Sergeant	Assault	Pickpocket
Clerk	Gown	Constable	Murder	Con Trick
Jury	Bible	Detective	Rape	Money Launder
Witness	Guilt	WPC	GBH	Scam
Usher	Innocence	Forensics	Strangle	Blackmail
Defendant	Autopsy	Station	Beat up	Bribery and
Plaintiff	.	Warrant Card	Fight	Corruption
Prosecutor	.	Notebook	Knuckle Duster	.
Defence Counsel	.	Truncheon	Knife	.
Magistrate	.	Whistle	Gun	.
Coroner	.	Handcuffs	Cudgel	.
.	.	.	.	.

PUNISHMENT	RELATIONSHIP	JEWELLERY	ROYALTY	MAIL
Execute	Husband	Diamond	Monarch	Letters
Hang	Wife	Sapphire	Emperor	Envelope
Gas	Parent	Ruby	Empress	Postcard
Lethal Injection	Child	Pearl	King	Greetings Card
Behead	Infant	Opal	Queen	Writing Pad
Convict	Son	Agate	Prince	Wrapping Paper
Prisoner	Daughter	Ring	Princess	String
Jail	Mother	Necklace	Duke	Sellotape
Incarcerate	Father	Broach	Duchess	Stamps
Whip	Brother	Tiara	Count	Parcel
Beat	Sister	Bracelet	Countess	Package
Manacles	Aunt	Earring	Earl	Parcel Tape
.	Uncle	Ring	Throne	Gift Tag
.	Nephew	.	Crown	Letterbox
.	Niece	.	Honours	Post Office
.	Legal Guardian	.	Knighthood	Postman
.	Step Parent	.	MBE	First Class
.	Grand Parent	.	CBE	Second Class
.	.	.	.	.

Logic List English: Meaningful Words - Volume 3

ARMY	RANK	HIERARCHY	CAMP	AIR FORCE
Artillery	Field Marshall	Division	CO	Air Commodore
Infantry	Chief of Staff	Regiment	Adjutant	Wing
Tank	General	Brigade	Orderly	Commander
Field Gun	Brigadier	Battalion	Cook	Squadron Leader
Anti-Tank Gun	Colonel	Platoon	Warrant Officer	Pilot Officer
Mortar	Major	Squad	Sentry Post	Bomber
Rifle	Captain	Paratroops	Guard Room	Fighter
Revolver	Lieutenant	Marines	Barracks	Jet
Automatic	Sergeant Major	Commandoes	Salute	Helicopter
Machine Gun	Sergeant	Engineers	Drill	Air-sea Rescue
Shell	Corporal	Sappers	Parade	Hangar
Rocket	Lance Corporal	Gunner	March	Landing Strip
Bullet	Lance	Sniper	Fall Out	Runway
Helmet	Bombardier	Binoculars	Attention	Conning Tower
Uniform	Private	Troop Carrier	Bayonet Practice	.
.	Medal	Jeep	Barbed Wire	.

NAVY	BOATS	TRANSPORT	VEHICLE PARTS	CAR INTERIOR
Admiral	Cruise Ship	Train	Chassis	Seat
Commander	Liner	Railway	Engine	Headrest
Captain	Ferry	Coach	Radiator	*Glove*
Lieutenant	Tugboat	Bus	Sump	*Compartment*
CPO	Yacht	Lorry	Starter Motor	Dashboard
Petty Officer	Paddle Steamer	Truck	Boot	Fuel Gauge
Able Seaman	Tanker	Artic	Bonnet	Dials
Stoker	Dredger	HGV	Wheels	Speedometer
Warship	Motor Boat	Van	Tyres	Handbrake
Aircraft Carrier	Trawler	Car	Exhaust	Foot Brake
Battleship	Speedboat	Motor	Hub Caps	Accelerator
Cruiser	Barge	Taxi	Headlights	Gears
Destroyer	Canal Boat	Cab	Indicators	Windscreen
Mine Sweeper	Rowing Boat	Motorbike	Bumpers	Wash
Support Vessel	Dingy	Scooter	Windscreen	Oil
Launch	Canoe	Bicycle	Wipers	Petrol
Submarine	.	Bike	.	Distilled Water
Periscope	.	Road	.	.
Depth Charge	.	Motorway	.	.
Mine	.	Path	.	.
.	.	Driver	.	.
.	.	Pedestrian	.	.

BUILDING WORK	WORK FORCE	SPORTS	ATHLETICS	COMBAT SPORTS
JCB	Site Manager	Football	Running	Martial Arts
Digger	Foreman	Rugby	Cross Country	Judo
Crane	Labourer	Basketball	Marathon	Karate
Steam Roller	Brick Layer	Cricket	Weight Lifting	Wrestling
Hoist	Builder	Tennis	Gymnastics	Boxing
Scaffold	Joiner	Badminton	Javelin	Fencing
Ladder	Tiler	Squash	Discus	Kendo
Planks	Plasterer	Polo	Hammer	.
Wheelbarrow	Plumber	Ice Hockey	High Jump	.
Shovel	Electrician	Archery	Long Jump	.
Sledge Hammer	Contractor	Shooting	Sprint	.
Pickaxe	Lorry Driver	Horse Racing	100 Metres	.
Trowel	.	Grand Prix	Pole Vault	.
Breeze Block	.	Pitch	Race Track	.
Cement Mixer	.	Field	Sports Ground	.
Concrete	.	Sports Club	Swimming Pool	.
.	.	.	.	.

SPORTSMEN	OUTDOOR PURSUITS	TREES	WILD PLANTS	GRASSES
Goalie	Hill Walking	Oak	Hawthorn	Rice
Goalkeeper	Hiking	Ash	Elder Bush	Rye
Defender	Mountaineering	Lime	Bramble	Wheat
Forward	Skiing	Sycamore	Dog Rose	Maize
Wing	Tobogganing	Maple	Thistle	Corn
Player	Ice Skating	Plane	Nettle	Barley
Bowler	Jogging	Chestnut	Foxglove	Oats
Batsman	Mountain Biking	Elm	Cow Parsley	Reed
Wicketkeeper	Orienteering	Beech	Bluebell	Bullrush
Umpire	Map Reading	Birch	Buttercup	Sedge
Referee	Bird Watching	Alder	Clover	.
Linesman	Foraging	Pine	Heather	.
Adjudicator	Scrambling	Conifer	Gorse	.
Fielder	Motocross	Cypress	Broom	.
.	Car Rally	Larch	Ivy	.
.	Rally Driving	Palm	.	.
.	Horse Riding	Monkey Puzzle	.	.
.	Caving	.	.	.

PLANT PARTS	FARMING	LIVESTOCK	PETS	BIG DOGS
Trunk	Tractor	Cattle	Cat	Boxer
Bark	Plough	Cows	Dog	Bulldog
Leaves	Combine	Pigs	Pony	Labrador
Twigs	Harvester	Swine	Goldfish	Great Dane
Branches	Harrow	Sheep	Parrot	Husky
Roots	Quad Bike	Goats	Budgie	Bloodhound
Stem	Trailer	Hens	Canary	Border Collie
Flowers	Barn	Ducks	Hamster	Springer
Bulbs	Milking Shed	Geese	Guinea Pig	St Bernard
Tubers	Stables	Turkeys	Vet	Dalmatian
.	Farmhouse	Eggs	.	Alsatian
.	Paddock	Market	.	Doberman
.	Fertilizer	.	.	Mastiff
.	Sheepdog	.	.	Rottweiler
.	Shotgun	.	.	Greyhound
.	Cartridge	.	.	Lurcher
.	.	.	.	Staffie*

SMALL DOGS	ACCESSORIES	LARGE ANIMALS	PREDATORS	MONKEYS
Poodle	Saddle	Elephant	Lion	Ape
Jack Russell	Halter	Rhino	Tiger	Gorilla
Border Terrier	Reins	Hippo	Jaguar	Orang-utan
Chihuahua	Stirrups	Giraffe	Leopard	Chimp
Pomeranian	Lead	Camel	Panther	Gibbon
Dachshund	Collar	Zebra	Cougar	Lemur
Pekinese	Perch	Horse	Hyena	.
Westie*	Swing	Donkey	Jackal	.
Scottie*	Bowl	Moose	Coyote	.
King Charles	Cage	Elk	Fox	.
Yorkie*	Hutch	Buffalo	Bear	.
Cocker Spaniel	Kennels	Deer	.	.
Corgi	.	Antelope	.	.
Terrier	.	Kangaroo	.	.

* These are common abbreviations for these breeds

REPTILES	SMALL ANIMALS	FLYING INSECTS	INSECTS ETC	MICROSCOPIC LIFE
Crocodile	Seal	Bee	Spider	Microbes
Alligator	Otter	Wasp	Millipede	Bacteria
Lizard	Stoat	Hornet	Centipede	Virus
Snake	Weasel	Fly	Earwig	Cells
Turtle	Rat	Moth	Woodlouse	Microscope
Tortoise	Bat	Butterfly	Scorpion	Slide
Terrapin	Mouse	Gnat	Beetle	.
Toad	Vole	Daddy-longlegs	Ant	.
Frog	Squirrel	Dragonfly	Flea	.
Newt	Hare	Mayfly	Tick	.
Tadpole	Rabbit	Mosquito	.	.
Cobra	.	Midge	.	.
Boa	.	.	.	.
Python	.	.	.	.
Viper	.	.	.	.
Anaconda	.	.	.	.
Frog Spawn	.	.	.	.

LARGE BIRDS	SMALL BIRDS	WATERBIRDS	SHELLFISH ETC	FRESHWATER FISH
Vulture	Blackbird	Swan	Cockles	Salmon
Eagle	Thrush	Goose	Mussels	Trout
Buzzard	Starling	Duck	Winkles	Pike
Falcon	Sparrow	Gull	Razor Shells	Chubb
Hawk	Robin	Wader	Snail	Carp
Raven	Wren	Heron	Slug	Rudd
Crow	Bullfinch	Egret	Worm	Roach
Rook	Chaffinch	Penguin	Sea Urchin	Perch
Jay	Swift	Tern	Starfish	Dace
Magpie	Swallow	Mallard	Jellyfish	Minnow
Jackdaw	House Martin	.	Squid	Stickleback
Pigeon	.	.	Octopus	Eel
Partridge	.	.	Crab	.
Pheasant	.	.	Lobster	.
Dove	.	.	Prawn	.
Woodpecker	.	.	Shrimp	.
.	.	.	Coral	.

FISH	LEGENDARY CREATURES	WEAPONS	ANCIENT PEOPLES	RELIGIONS
Whale	Dragon	Sword	Maya	Islam
Shark	Unicorn	Spear	Inca	Christianity
Swordfish	Phoenix	Lance	Aztec	Hinduism
Marlin	Cyclops	Dagger	Roman	Catholicism
Dolphin	Minotaur	Shield	Gaul	Sikhism
Porpoise	Monster	Axe	Celt	Buddhism
Tuna	Werewolf	Battle-axe	Anglo-Saxon	Paganism
Cod	Vampire	Mace	Norman	Agnosticism
Haddock	Zombie	Chain Mace	Viking	Atheism
Dogfish	.	Armour	Goth	Heaven
Herring	.	Crossbow	Vandal	Paradise
Sardines	.	Bow & Arrow	Mongol	Morality
Anchovies	.	.	Barbarian	Spirituality
Whiting	.	.	Warrior	.
Angel Fish	.	.	.	.

CASTLE	CREATURE PARTS	HEAD ACTIONS	ANIMAL MOTION	MYTHICAL BEINGS
Keep	Paws	Sniff	Sit	Sorcerer
Dungeon	Fangs	Snort	Stand	Wizard
Torture Chamber	Whiskers	Snore	Lie Down	Witch
Drawbridge	Hooves	Blink	Walk	Warlock
Portcullis	Horns	Swallow	Run	Fairy
Moat	Snout	Chew	Gallop	Dwarf
Tower	Muzzle	Lick	Jump	Elf
Banqueting Hall	Tusk	Howl	Swing	Goblin
Courtyard	Wings	Bark	Swim	Genie
Battlements	Beak	Squeal	Slither	Devil
Catapult	Claws	.	Swoop	Demon
Siege Engine	Fur	.	Dig	God
Armoury	Feathers	.	Burrow	Goddess
.	Shell	.	Hop	Hero
.	Spines	.	Crawl	.
.	Tail	.	.	.
.	Fin	.	.	.
.	Scales	.	.	.
.	Gills	.	.	.
.	Fluke	.	.	.

SECTION TWO
PROPER NOUNS

Logic List English: Meaningful Words - Volume 3

FAMOUS CARS	MOTORBIKES ETC.	FOOTBALL TEAMS	LONDON LANDMARKS	NATIONAL LANDMARKS
Ford	Yamaha	*Manchester - United*	Buckingham -Palace	Windsor Castle
Fiat	Kawasaki	Manchester City	Tower Bridge	*Edinburgh - Castle*
Mercedes	Norton	Leeds	*Houses of - Parliament*	The Royal Mile
Audi	Bonneville	Liverpool	*Tower of - London*	*Blackpool - Tower*
Chevrolet	BSA Bantam	Arsenal	*Natural History -Museum*	*Blackpool - Illuminations*
Rolls Royce	*Harley -Davidson*	Aston Villa	Planetarium	Arundel Castle
Bentley	Lambretta	Everton	Madame Tussauds	*Greenwich - Observatory*
Aston Martin	Vespa	Chelsea	*Victoria And - Albert*	*The Royal - Pavilion*
Alfa Romeo	Scooter	West Ham	Science Museum	Falkirk Wheel
Lamborghini	Moped	QPR	Globe Theatre	.
Jaguar	.	*Sheffield* - Wednesday*	Leicester Square	.
Maserati	.	Crystal Palace	*Piccadilly - Square*	.
Vauxhall	.	*Hull Kingston - Rovers*	Soho	.
Lotus Elan	.	Rangers	HMS Victory	.
Mini	.	Celtic	*Westminster - Abbey*	.
Volvo	.	Hearts	The Albert Hall	.
Peugeot	.		Kew Gardens	
Citroen	.		London Zoo	
Volkswagen	.			

FAMOUS SHOPS	HOTELS ETC	BANKS	HISTORICAL FIGURES	POLITICAL FIGURES
Harrods	Claridges	*Bank of -England*	Julius Caesar	Washington
Selfridges	The Carlton	*Clydesdale -Bank*	Attila The Hun	Lincoln
Marks & Spencers	The Ritz	*Royal Bank of - Scotland*	Alfred The Great	Truman
BHS	*Trusthouse -Forte*	Bank of Scotland	*William The - Conqueror*	Roosevelt
Debenhams	Marriot Hotels	Barclays	King John	Bismark
Boots	Warner Hotels	Lloyds	*Richard The - Lionheart*	Kaiser Wilhelm
WH Smith	Expedia Hotels	TSB	Cortez	Stalin
Tesco	Travel Lodges	.	Montezuma	Hitler
Morrisons	Premier Inn	.	Charlemagne	Churchill
Sainsburys	Youth Hostel	.		Castro
Asda	YMCA	.		Kennedy
TK Maxx	.	.		Khrushchev
B&Q	*Highlighted sections equal phrase spread over more than one line	.		.
Halfords		.		.
Homebase		.		.
Amazon		.		.
Co-op		.		.

Logic List English: Meaningful Words - Volume 3

MILITARY FIGURES	FAMOUS MUSICALS	FAMOUS AUTHORS	SPORTS VENUES	FAMOUS ACTORS
Nelson	Oliver	Emily Bronte	White City	Clark Gable
Napoleon	*Barber of Seville*	Charlotte Bronte	Newmarket	Gary Cooper
Wellington	Rigoletto	Jane Austen	*Madison Square Gardens*	Lon Chaney
Drake	Carmen	Thomas Hardy	Wembley	Charlton Heston
Rommel	*The Magic Flute*	Leo Tolstoy	Wimbledon	James Stewart
Montgomery	Pirates of Penzance	Oscar Wilde	Twickenham	James Cagney
Eisenhower	Madam Butterfly	Camus	The Oval	Humphrey Bogart
Patton	The Ring Cycle	Dostoyevsky	Lords	Cary Grant
Zhukov	La Traviata	Shakespeare	Brands Hatch	Burt Lancaster
.	La Boheme	Noel Coward	Glen Eagles	*Arnold Schwarzenegger*
.	Tosca	Tennessee Williams	.	Kirk Douglas
.		Edgar Allen Poe	.	.
.		HG Wells	.	.
.		Agatha Christie	.	
.		DH Lawrence		

FAMOUS BOOKS	BATTLES	FAMOUS FILMS	CHILDREN'S AUTHORS	SPORTS EVENTS
Jane Eyre	Waterloo	Casablanca	JK Rowland	Royal Ascot
Wuthering Heights	Agincourt	Ben Hur	Roald Dahl	Grand National
Pride & Prejudice	Crecy	Psycho	Enid Blyton	The Ashes
Alice in Wonderland	Bosworth Field	The Lady Vanishes	*The Brothers Grimm*	League Cup
Doctor Zhivago	Edge Hill	Zulu	Lewis Carroll	Tour De France
Oliver Twist	Culloden	Goldfinger	*Hans Christian Anderson*	Olympics
Little Women	The Somme	*Gone with the Wind*	CS Lewis	*Commonwealth Games*
War and Peace	Stalingrad	Alien	Jules Verne	Ladbrokes
Far from the Madding Crowd	The Bulge	Star Wars	.	William Hill
Lord of the Rings	Normandy	*Good, the Bad and the Ugly*	.	Coral

FICTIONAL CHARACTERS	FAMOUS SPORTSMEN	BRITISH ACTORS	FAMOUS SINGERS	BAND LEADERS
Sherlock - Holmes	Stirling Moss	Laurence Olivier	Frank Sinatra	Glen Miller
Dr Watson	Muhammed Ali	John Gielgud	Dean Martin	Tommy Dorsey
Dracula	Cassius Clay	*Ralph - Richardson*	Bobby Darin	Benny Goodman
Frankenstein	George Best		Elvis Presley	Kenny Ball
James Bond	Bobby Moore	*Michael - Redgrave*	Sammy Davis	Acker Bilk
Philip Marlow	Bobby Charlton		Ella Fitzgerald	Duke Ellington
Allan - Quartermain	Pele	John Mills	Bing Crosby	Louis Armstrong
	David Beckham	Sean Connery	Billie Holiday	Kenny Barber
Harry Potter	Henry Cooper	Michael Caine	Edith Piaf	Humphrey Littleton
Noddy	Graham Hill	Basil Rathbone	Judy Garland	
Gandalf	Fred Perry	Richard Burton	Lena Horne	Johnny Dankworth
Captain Nemo	.	Alec Guinness	Shirley Bassey	
.	.	David Niven	Tony Bennet	.
.	.	*Richard - Attenborough*	.	.

FAMOUS ACTRESSES	FAMOUS PLAYS	BRITISH ACTRESSES	FAMOUS COMEDIANS	UK COMEDIANS
Greta Garbo	MacBeth	Peggy Ashcroft	Bob Hope	Spike Milligan
Gloria Swanson	Julius Caesar	*Cybil - Thorndyke*	Jack Benny	Tommy Cooper
Betty Davis	Hamlet		Peter Sellers	Ken Dodd
Lana Turner	*Midsummer - Nights Dream*	Judi Dench	Joan Rivers	Tommy Trinder
Jayne Mansfield		Maggie Smith	Laurel & Hardy	Arthur Askey
Sophia Loren	Romeo & Juliet	Diana Dors	Harold Lloyd	Kenneth Williams
Bridget Bardo	*Much Ado - About Nothing*	Julie Christie	Charlie Chaplin	
Elizabeth Taylor		Susannah York	Buster Keaton	Sid James
Katherine Hepburn	Amadeus	Emma Thompson	Abbot & Costello	Frankie Howerd
	The Cherry - Orchard		The 3 Stooges	Benny Hill
Audrey Hepburn		Helen Mirren	Dick van Dyke	Monty Python
Joan Crawford	Uncle Vanya	Sheila Hancock	Lenny Bruce	Cannon & Ball
Joan Fontaine	*Long Days - Journey into - Night*	Maureen Lipman	Jimmy Durante	The 2 Ronnies
		Kathleen Harrison	Woody Allen	Eric Sykes
	Under Milk - Wood	Hermoine Gingold		Hattie Jacques
				Morecambe & - Wise

POP GROUPS	FAMOUS ARTISTS	POP SINGERS	FAMOUS COMPOSERS
Beatles	Picasso	Bob Dylan	Beethoven
Rolling Stones	Cezanne	Pete Seeger	Handel
Beach Boys	Monet	Tom Paxton	Strauss
Byrds	Degas	Johnny Cash	Bach
Kinks	Van Gogh	*Michael Jackson*	Stravinsky
The Who	Toulouse Lautrec	Frank Iffield	Vaughan Williams
Led Zepplin	Matisse	Roy Orbison	Tchaikovsky
Mamas & Papas	Renoir	*Dusty Springfield*	Sibelius
Pink Floyd	Michael Angelo	Tom Jones	Delius
Queen	Titian	Lulu	Delibes
U2	*Leonardo Da Vinci*	Cilla Black	Holst
Monkees	Rubens		Mozart
Supremes	Rembrandt		Schubert
	Constable		Chopin
	Andy Warhol		Liszt
			Wagner

INDEX

Abandon 46	Adhere 47	Alter 47	Aristocrat 47	Awe 47
Abbot 46	Adjoin 47	Alternate 22	Arithmetic 22	Awkward 47
Abhor 46	Adjust 27	Amalgam 47	Arm 16	Back 18, 47
Able 10	Admire 22	Amatuer 12	Arrange 18	Bag 28
Abolish 27	Admit 27, 12	Amaze 37	Arrogance 22	Bake 47
Abominate 36	Adore 27	Ambiguous 28	Art 37	Balance 45
Abort 36	Adopt 47	Ambition 37	Artful 47	Bald 47
Abrade 46	Adroit 36	Amity 18	Argue 28	Baptism 47
Abrupt 46	Adult 36	Amorous 37	Articulate 26	Barbarian 28
Absent 12	Advance 16	Amplify 37	Artificial 47	Baron 37
Absolute 27	Adventure 31	Amuse 47	Ascend 18	Base 27, 28
Absorb 27	Adverse 47	Anaesthesia 22	Assassin 47	Bath 37
Abstain 22	Advert 36	Analyse 28	Assemble 15	Battle 20
Abstract 46	Advice 22	Anarchy 28	Assert 47	Beast 48
Absurd 46	Aerate 27	Anatomy 47	Assess 37	Beauty 22
Abundant 46	Aerial 27	Ancestor 47	Assist 47	Becoming 47
Abuse 27	Aerospace 27	Angel 47	Associate 40	Beg 47
Abyss 46	Aesthetic 36	Anger 47	Assume 16	Begin 48
Academy 46	Affect 10	Angle 47	Astound 37	Behave 37
Accelerate 29	Affection 16	Animate 18	Astrology 47	Belief 18
Accent 36	Affirm 27	Announce 11	Astronomy 18	Bend 47
Accept 36	Afflict 34	Annual 37	Astute 28	Benefit 13
Access 22	Age 37	Anonymity 47	Atheism 18	Betray 16
Accident 18	Agent 47	Antagonize 28	Athlete 37	Bewilder 47
Accommodate 46	Aggression 22	Antique 37	Atom 28	Bide 28
Accomplish 36	Aggrevate 47	Anxiety 47	Atrocity 47	Bide 46
Account 22, 46	Agitate 47	Apathy 28	Attack 35	Bigot 48
Accumulate 27	Agony 47	Apology 47	Attain 47	Bind 48
Accurate 26	Agree 40	Appeal 47	Attention 47	Biography 28
Accuse 27	Agreeable 51	Appear 22	Attract 14	Biology 28
Achieve 46	Ail 47	Appetite 37	Audacity 47	Bisect 34
Acid 36	Aim 47	Apply 37	Aural 16	Bitch 48
Acoustic 46	Air 37	Appreciate 47, 51	Auspicious 34	Bitter 32
Acquaint 36	Alarm 47		Authentic 37	Black 48
Acquire 16	Alcohol 47	Approach 37	Author 47	Blaspheme 37
Acrid 46	Alien 37	Appropriate 37	Authority 28	Blaze 36
Acrobat 46	Allege 37	Approve 37	Autocracy 47	Bless 48
Act 36	Allergy 47	Approximate 28	Automate 37	Block 48
Acute 36	Ally 37	Apt 26	Available 47	Blood 37
Adapt 47	Allot 37	Arbitrate 37	Avenge 21	Blot 48
Add 16	Allow 37	Arch 47	Avoid 37	Blow 37
Addict 36	Alone 27	Archaic 37	Awake 37	Board 48
Adequate 26	Alphabet 47	Architect 47	Aware 37	

Body 32
Bold 32
Bomb 37
Booze 48
Bounds 36
Bowl 48
Box 48
Brains 48
Brash 48
Brave 48
Break 28
Breath 28
Breed 18
Brew 48
Brief 51
Bright 12
Broad 37
Brother 38
Brute 22
Build 34
Bulb 38
Bulge 38
Bumble 48
Bungle 48
Buoy 48
Bureau 38
Burgle 48
Bursar 51
Calculate 21
Calm 37
Camp 25
Cancer 30
Capture 14
Category 30
Cause 30
Caution 24
Cave 30
Cease 26
Celebrate 41
Censor 30
Centralize 41
Century 30
Ceremony 53

Certain 24
Certify 30
Change 27, 41
Character 24
Cheek 41
Cheer 41
Chemist 22
Chronology 18
Cinema 53
Circle 13
Civic 30
Civility 53
Claim 38
Class 41
Clean 24
Cleave 41
Cleric 41
Climate 36
Climax 47
Close 14
Cloth 41
Coarse 41
Coast 41
Cocky 41
Code 19
Cognizance 24
Cohere 18
Coincide 41
Collaborate 41
Collect 24
Colony 24
Colour 23
Combat 41
Comfort 40
Comic 30
Command 41
Commence 54
Commend 29
Common 41
Commune 41
Communicate 17, 22
Company 41

Compare 22, 24
Compatible 45
Compensate 49
Compete 41
Competent 45
Complete 19
Complex 35
Comprehend 37
Compute 30
Calcium 53
Can 53
Candid 53
Cannibal 53
Canon 53
Captive 53
Cardiac 53
Catalyst 53
Caustic 53
Ceremony 53
Challenge 53
Chance 53
Chapel 53
Charity 53
Chasten 53
Chauvenism 53
Child 53
Chlorine 53
Clarity 53
Classic 53
Clear 53
Clever 53
Clip 53
Close 53
Cloud 53
Clumsy 53
Coagulate 53
Code 53
Coerce 53
Cold 53
Commentate 53
Commerce 53
Compact 53
Company 18

Compile 53
Complain 53
Compose 53
Conceal 53
Concede 54
Conceive 41
Concept 13, 14
Concern 41
Conciliate 19
Concise 12
Conclude 26, 30
Condemn 54
Condense 54
Condition 38
Conduct 30
Cone 54
Confection 54
Confess 41
Confide 24
Confine 54
Confirm 27
Conform 41
Confuse 41
Congratulate 54
Congregate 24
Congress 54
Congruent 34
Connect 16
Conquer 41
Conscience 54
Conscious 19
Consequence 34
Conserve 16
Consider 15
Consist 41
Console 54
Conspicuous 54
Conspire 41
Constant 34
Constituent 19
Constrict 19
Construct 29
Consul 54

Consult 30
Consume 41
Contact 54
Contain 54
Contaminate 30
Contemplate 54
Contempt 54
Contend 41
Content 29
Contest 54
Continent 43, 34
Continue 11
Contort 30
Contract 24
Contradict 54
Contrary 41
Contribute 41
Contrite 54
Contive 54
Control 30
Controversy 44
Convalesce 54
Convene 54
Convenient 15
Conventional 54
Converge 41
Converse 30
Convert 41
Convince 54
Convulse 54
Cook 41
Cool 31
Cooperate 41
Coordinate 41
Curious 34
Corporate 34
Corpse 22
Correct 31
Correlate 54
Correspond 41
Corroborate 54
Corrugate 54
Corrupt 3

Cosmic 35
Cost 42
Cosy 42
Courage 20
Courtesy 24
Coward 42
Crack 42
Craft 42
Crafty 35
Crass 42
Crazy
Create 35
Cremate 42
Credit 13
Crime 13
Crisp 42
Critic 24
Cross 35, 47
Crown 41
Crude 42
Cruel 42
Crumb 42
Crust 32
Cryptic 31
Crystal 42
Culprit 42
Cultivate 26
Culture 24
Cunning 35
Curb 31
Cure 35
Current 54
Curse 46
Curt 31
Curve 35
Custody 42
Custom 35
Cut 24
Cute 42
Cycle 35
Cynic 35
Damp 39
Danger 32

Dark 15
Daunt 51
Dazzle
Dead 29
Deaf 51
Deal 51
Dear 20
Debt 34
Deceive 16
Decent 26
Decide 29
Decimal 51
Decorate 29
Decorum 51
Dedicate 51
Deduce 29
Deep 29
Defeat 29
Defect 39
Defend 14
Defer 51
Deficit 51
Define 18
Deflect 51
Defoliate 51
Deft 51
Defy 39
Degenerate 51
Deity 51
Dejected 51
Delicate 26
Delirious 51
Deliver 51
Demented 51
Democracy 39
Demolish 51
Demon 39
Demonstrate 29, 39
Demote 39
Dense 39
Dental 39
Deny 39

Depart 51, 54
Dependent 15
Deposit 39
Deprecate 51
Depress 29
Deprive 29
Deputy 51
Deride 29
Derive 51
Dermatitis 51
Descend 18, 51
Describe 26
Desert 51
Deserve 40
Desire 29
Despair 19
Despise 51
Despot 51
Destiny 40
Destroy 29
Detect 40, 51
Determine 22
Determined 40
Detest 51
Detonate 51
Devastate 51
Develop 16
Deviate 40
Devil 23
Devious 51
Devote 51
Devout 29
Dexterity 37
Diagnose 51
Diagram 25
Dictate 51
Dictator 40
Diet 40
Differ 23
Digest 15
Digit 51
Dignity 34, 40
Digress 51

Diligent 51
Dim 12
Dine 40
Diplomacy 51
Direct 11, 40
Dirt 51
Disaster 51
Discern 40
Discipline 52
Discover 23
Discreet 22
Discriminate 23
Disease 12
Disguise 45
Dispense 22
Disperse 46
Dispose 26
Disposed 40
Dispute 34
Disrupt 29
Dissect 34
Dissent 52
Dissolve 34
Distant 33
Distil 30
Distinct 23
Distinguish 40
Distress 40
Distribute 52
Disturb 23
Dither 40
Diverse 40
Divert 52
Divide 11, 30
Divine 52
Dizzy 52
Docile 52
Doctor 52
Doctrine 26
Document 52
Doddery 52
Dogged 40
Dogma 40

Domestic 30
Domicile 52
Dominate 18
Donate 52
Dope 30
Double 49
Doubt 15
Dowdy 52
Doze 30
Drama 16
Draper 52
Draught 52
Draw 30
Dream 52
Dreary 52
Dregs 52
Dress 23
Drift 36
Drizzle 52
Drop 40
Drunk 23
Dry 40
Duel 52
Duke 30
Dull 40
Duplicate 23
Duration 52
Dusty 40
Dwell 52
Dynamic 40
Eager 44
Earth 31
Ease 12
East 32
Eat 25
Ecology 44
Economy 17
Edge 32
Edit 32
Educate 25
Effect 10
Ego 20
Eject 17

Elect 25	Event 25	Fabricate 23	Firm 22, 48	Frenzy 19
Electric 10	Evidence 33	Face 25, 48	Fit 28, 38, 48	Frequent 38
Element 44	Evolve 33	Facile 48	Five 19	Fresh 18
Eligible 46	Exact 20	Fail 48	Fix 27	Friend 16
Eloquent 44	Exaggerate 44	Fair 28	Fizz 38	Fright 28
Embark 40	Exam 33	Faith 23	Flame 27	Frill 38
Embryo 33	Example 44	Fallible 34	Flat 51	Fringe 38
Emerge 36	Excavate 44	False 13	Flatter 48	Frisk 48
Eminent 25	Exceed 25	Fame 18	Flavour 48	Frivolous 48
Emit 12	Except 25	Familiar 28	Flaw 48	Front 25
Emphasis 32	Excess 44	Fan 38	Flex 38	Frost 28
Empire 18	Excite 33	Fancy 38	Flippant 48	Frugal 49
Employ 20	Exclaim 33	Farce 48	Flirt 48	Fruit 28
Enchant 25	Excuse 44	Fascinate 48	Float 47	Frustrate 38
End 32	Execute 20	Fashion 48	Flower 48	Fumes 49
Endemic 44	Exhale 20	Fat 48	Fluctuate 34	Fun 49
Endure 32	Exhaust 25	Fatal 48	Fluent 27	Function 48, 51
Energy 32	Exhibit 17	Fate 38	Fluid 46	Fundamental 38
Engage 25	Exist 13	Fathom 48	Fold 48	Fungus 49
Engrave 32	Expand 33	Fatuous 27	Follow 48	Fur 49
Enrol 44	Expect 33	Fault 28	Fool 23	Furnace 46
Enter 32	Expedite 33	Favourable 23	Force 13	Furnish 38
Enthuse 25	Expel 41	Feasible 48	Forest 16	Further 49
Entire 44	Experiment 33	Feather 48	Forge 48	Fury 34. 49
Envelop 17	Expert 46	Federal 30	Form 19	Fuse 49
Environment 33	Expire 21	Feeble 25	Formal 28	Fuss 38
Epidermis 33	Explain 21	Female 17	Formula 48	Gallant 45
Equal 11	Explode 21	Fence 48	Fornicate 48	Game 21
Equity 34	Exploit 44	Fertile 38	Fort 38	Gang 45
Equivocal 44	Export 17	Fertilize 48	Fortune 19	Garden 45
Erase 22	Expound 21	Festive 48	Fossil 48	Gas 45
Erode 33	Express 14	Fever 38	Found 48	Gastric 26
Error 33	Expression 26	Fibre 48	Four 16	Gather 45
Escalate 44	Extent 26	Fiction 28	Fraction 48	Gaudy 45
Escape 20	Exterior 21	Fiddle 48	Fracture 48	Gender 21
Essence 43	Extinct 33	Fiend 48	Fragile 48	Gene 15
Esteem 25	Extinguish 33	Fierce 28	Franchise 32	General 26
Eternal 44	Extortion 44	Fight 46	Frank 48	Generate 39
Ethics 33	Extravagant 45	Fill 48	Frantic 19	Generous 45
Euphemism 44	Extreme 33	Filth 38	Fraternal 38	Genial 41
Evacuate 44	Extricate 46	Final 14	Fraud 51	Genius 46
Evade 44	Extrovert 33	Finance 28	Free 48	Gentle 17
Evangelism 33	Fabled 48	Fine 48	Freeze 23	Genuine 14

Geology 21	Grumble 21	Hot 26	Include 13	Integrity 27
Geriatric 45	Guarantee 45	Hotel 33	Increase 34	Intellect 13
Germ 45	Guard 17	House 49	Incubate 45	Intelligence 13
Germinate 45	Guilt 33	Human 26	Indicate 34	Intend 34
Gesture 45	Gun 33	Humane 15	Indolence 22	Intent 13
Ghost 33	Gymnasium 33	Humid 26	Induce 26	Inter 52
Ghoul 33	Gyrate 26	Humiliate 45	Indulge 46	Interest 27
Glad 33	Habit 21	Humour 45	Industrial 22	Interfere 34
Glamour 45	Habitat 21	Hunger 45	Inebriate 46	Interior 21
Glare 45	Hair 45	Hunt 45	Inert 46	Intermittent 46
Glass 21	Hallucinate 33	Hydrate 29	Inevitable 46	Intern 46
Gleam 17	Hand 12	Hyphen 45	Infant 34	Interpret 34
Glide 45	Happy 45	Hypnosis 26	Infect 27	Interrogate 34
Globe 26	Harass 45	Hypocrisy 45	Inferior 34	Interrupt 29
Gloom 17	Harmonics 12	Hysteria 45	Infiltrate 46	Intimate 46
Glory 21	Harmony 12	Ice 18	Infinite 27	Intricate 46
Gloss 45	Harsh 45	Icon 45	Inflame 34	Introduce 11
Glow 47	Haste 33	Ideal 11	Inflate 28, 29, 34	Introvert 33
Glue 45	Hate 45	Idenity 26	Inflict 34	Intrude 21
Go 33	Haul 45	Ignite 45	Inform 11	Intuition 34
God 33	Hazard 33	Ignominy 45	Ingenuous 46	Invade 46
Good 33	Head 21	Ignore 26	Inhale 20	Invent 15
Govern 17	Heal 26	Illusion 18	Initiate 22	Invert 35
Grade 13	Hear 45	Illustrate 45	Inject 22	Invest 46
Grain 21	Heart 21	Image 13	Injure 46	Investigate 35
Grand 21	Heat 33	Imitate 26	Innocence 34	Invincible 46
Graphic 21	Heavy 33	Immediate 45	Insect 46	Invite 35
Grasp 45	Help 33	Immune 21	Inside 34	Involve 46
Grate 45	Herb 21	Impel 17	Insinuate 46	Irony 45
Grateful 13	Heredity 21	Impetuous 45	Insist 15	Irrate 45
Gratis 45	Heresy 45	Imply 26	Insolent 46	Irritate 26
Gravity 15	Hero 21	Impose 26	Inspect 27	Island 34
Great 33	Hesitate 21	Impressionism 26	Inspire 21	Isolate 34
Greed 33	High 33		Instant 46	Jelly 20
Green 21	Hill 33	Idiot 33	Instigate 46	Join 32
Grey 45	History 18	Idle 33	Instinct 46	Joy 10
Grief 31	Hoard 45	Idol 33	Institute 34	Judge 10
Grim 45	Honest 26	In 10	Instruction 34	Juvenile 46
Grime 45	Honour 21	Inaugerate 45	Instrument 34	Kind 25
Grip 45	Horizon 45	Incident 18	Insubordinate 46	Know 20
Grit 45	Horror 18	Incinerate 45	Insulate 46	Labour 46
Ground 45	Hospital 33	Inclined 40	Insure 17	Lancet 27
Grub 45	Host 26	Incise 12	Insurrection 46	Land 10

Languish 35	Machine 49	Meteor 49	Move 16	Nurse 44
Large 20	Mad 28	Meteorology 49	Mug 49	Obey 14
Last 22	Magic 38	Method 23	Multiple 28	Object 32
Late 22	Magnanimous 49	Microbe 28	Murder 49	Objective 31
Laudable 35	Magnet 28	Middle 28	Music 23	Oblige 17
Laugh 46	Magnificent 49	Might 37	Musket 49	Oblique 44
Launder 46	Magnify 49	Migrate 12	Mutate 16	Obscene 32
Law 15	Majesty 49	Mild 49	Mute 23	Observe 14
Lazy 35	Make 38	Military 16	Mutiny 49	Obstinate 44
Lead 35. 46	Male 17	Million 49	Mystery 14	Obtrude 44
Learn 35	Man 19	Mind 38, 49	Myth 38	Obverse 54
Leg 35	Manage 23	Minister 20	Naked 25	Occasion 44
Legal 10	Mania 38	Minor 38	Name 12	Occlude 44
Length 12	Manipulate 38	Minute 28	Narrate 32	Occupied 52
Letter 46	Margin 49	Miracle 49	Narrow 32	Occupy 20
Liberal 27	Marine 38	Mischief 49	Nasty 44	Occur 29
Liberty 22	Marry 18	Miser 49	Nation 12	Odd 44
Light 15, 20, 47	Mason 49	Misery 53	Nature 11	Odour 17
Like 22, 35	Master 38	Mist 49	Navigate 25	Offend 32
Limit 35	Maternal 28	Mix 27	Navy 32	Office 17
Lingual 46	Matter 13	Mobile 19	Need 12	Oil 32
Liquid 22	Mature 28	Modern 28	Negate 12	One 32
Liquidate 35	Maximum 28	Modest 12	Neighbour 32	Open 32
Literate 13	Mean 38	Modify 23	Nerve 14, 25	Operate 25
Live 14	Measure 28	Moist 38	Neutral 44	Opinion 44
Loathe 46	Mechanic 23	Molest 49	New 12	Opponent 44
Local 12	Medal 49	Moment 38	Nice 32	Opportunity 25
Lofty 27	Meddle 49	Monarch 49	Night 20	Oppose 19
Logical 21	Mediate 49	Money 19	Nip 44	Optic 17
Lonely 27	Medicine 16	Monk 28	Nitrogen 44	Optimum 13
Long 35, 46	Meditation 38	Monocle 38	Noble 25	Oral 17
Loose 18	Meek 49	Monogamy 37	Node 25	Orchestra 32
Lose 46	Melancholy 49	Monotone 38	Normal 18	Order 25
Loud 35	Melody 28	Monster 38	North 25	Ordinary 32
Love 15	Member 53	Mood 49	Nose 32	Organ 32
Low 35	Memory 12	Moral 15	Note 13, 37	Organise 25
Loyal 27	Mend 25	Morale 51	Notorious 44	Orient 20
Lubricate 46	Menopause 23	Mortal 15	Nourish 16	Origin 17
Lucid 27	Merchant 49	Most 47	Novel 44	Ornament 32
Luck 27	Merit 38	Motion 14	Nuclear 32	Orphan 44
Luminous 18	Merry 49	Motive 49	Nude 25	Oscillate 44
Lure 47	Mess 49	Mountain 28	Nullify 47	
Luxury 27	Metaphor 49	Mourn 38	Number 11	

Osseous 44	Peril 45	Point 52	Prison 34	Pursue 53
Ostensible 32	Period 52	Poison 52	Private 16	Push 53
Our 44	Perish 52	Pole 40	Process 53	Putrid 30
Out 10	Permanent 40	Polite 43	Procrastinate 52	Puzzle 53
Outrage 32	Permeate 52	Politics 21	Procure 53	Quake 33
Outside 34	Permit 40	Pollute 52	Professional 12	Qualify 19
Ova 17	Perpetrate 52	Pomp 23	Profit 41	Quantity 43
Overt 32	Perpetual 40	Ponderous 34	Program 53	Query 43
Own 32	Persecute 52	Poor 34	Progress 23	Quiet 25
Oxygen 32	Personal 33	Pope 30	Prohibit 24	Quiz 13
Pack 30	Personality 18	Popular 30	Project 22	Quote 25
Pacifist 40	Persuade 40	Populate 19	Projector 53	Race 38
Paint 52	Pertain 26	Porter 52	Prolific 53	Radiate 21
Palate 52	Perturb 45	Portray 52	Prominent 53	Radical 49
Palings 52	Pervade 33	Pose 52	Prompt 41, 45	Rage 32
Palpable 33	Pervert 30	Possess 14	Propel 53	Ram 32
Panel 52	Pessimism 13	Possible 11	Proper 26	Rapid 38
Paradox 52	Pharmacy 30	Post 52	Prophet 41	Rare 38
Paralyse 40	Philanthropy 52	Potent 21	Proportion 29	Rational 15
Parasite 36	Philosophy 40	Pothole 52	Propose 19	React 29
Pardon 52	Phonetic 40	Powder 52	Proscribe 24	Read 29
Parent 40	Phosphate 40	Power 25	Prosecute 20	Real 11
Parley 52	Photograph 23	Practical 18	Prosper 53	Reason 29
Parson 23	Physical 49	Practice 49	Protect 30	Rebel 19
Part 30	Picture 40	Precise 12	Protract 53	Receive 23
Partial 33	Pirate 52	Predict 40	Prove 41, 52	Reciprocol 29
Participate 40	Pity 40	Predominant 52	Provide 53	Recite 49
Pass 15	Place 23, 32	Prefer 30	Providence 53	Reckless 49
Passion 13	Placid 26	Pregnant 21	Province 53	Reckon 49
Paternal 30	Plain 52	Prepare 30	Proviso 53	Recognize 38
Pathology 52	Plan 52	Prescribe 52	Provoke 53	Record 38
Pathos 17	Planet 34	Present 12	Prude 53	Recover 51
Patience 26	Plant 26, 51	President 52	Prudent 53	Rectify 49
Patriot 15	Plausible 40	Pretence 14	Psyche 53	Recuperate 38
Pay 23, 40	Play 34	Pretty 52	Psychiatry 11	Red 38
Peace 30	Please 12	Prevail 40	Psychosis 41	Redeem 21
Pedant 52	Plenty 52	Prevent 30	Public 16	Reduce 34
Penal 16	Pliant 19	Pride 40	Publicize 53	Refer 49
Penetrate 33	Plod 52	Priest 40	Publish 41	Refine 29
Pension 52	Pluck 52	Prime 24	Pulse 41	Reflect 39
Perceive 26	Plumb 52	Prince 40	Punch 24	Reform 49
Perfect 18	Plunge 52	Principal 24	Punish 41	Refute 34
Perform 52	Poem 40	Print 49	Puppet 53	Regard 49

Regent 19	Retard 50	Saliva 42	Sensuous 15	Skin 42
Regiment 49	Retire 50	Salutary 46	Sentient 10	Slack 36
Register 49	Retract 50	Sample 42	Separate 19	Slave 20
Regress 23	Retrieve 39	Sane 27	Sequel 24	Sleep 24
Regret 49	Retrograde 50	Sanitary 46	Serene 42	Slip 42
Regular 14	Return 50	Sarcasm 35	Series 42	Slow 24
Reject 17	Reveal 53	Sate 14	Serious 42	Slug 42
Related 23	Revere 15	Satire 35	Serve 17	Smart 36
Relax 29	Revert 20	Saturate 42	Settle 42	Smoke 31
Relief 37	Revive 39	Sauce 42	Seven 24	Snap 42
Religion 39	Revoke 34	Savage 42	Severe 42	Sneak 42
Reluctant 49	Rhetoric 50	Save 35	Sewage 42	Snob 36
Rely 19	Rheumatism 39	Scab 35	Sex 24	Sober 23
Remain 49	Rhythm 39	Scandal 42	Shabby 42	Sociable 36
Remark 49	Rich 25	Scant 35	Shade 35	Society 11
Reminisce 49	Ride 16	Scarce 42	Shake 42	Soft 24
Renounce 39	Right 19	Scene 35	Shallow 35	Solemn 42
Repair 26	Rigid 50	Sceptic 35	Shame 40	Solicitor 42
Repeat 19	Rise 37, 50	Schizophrenia 42	Shape 38, 42	Solid 31
Repel 41	Risk 50	School 31	Sharp 35	Solitary 42
Repent 39	Rite 39	Science 31	Shave 42	Soluble 30
Replicate 23	Robot 50	Scot 35	Sheep 31	Solve 27
Report 39	Robust 50	Scribe 22	Shelf 42	Solvent 34
Represent 49	Rock 50	Scrupulous 35	Shine 42	Somnolent 22
Reproach 45	Romance 23	Sculpt 31	Ship 42	Sophist 42
Republic 50	Rotate 39	Seam 35	Shock 42	Sophisticated 36
Repulse 14	Rough 29	Search 39	Short 42	Sour 42
Repute 19	Rouse 37	Season 35	Show 42	South 31
Resent 50	Royal 39	Seclude 42	Shrewd 28	Space 43
Reserve 50	Rubber 50	Secret 24	Shrill 42	Spark 36
Reside 39	Rude 23, 50	Secretary 42	Sick 24	Sparse 42
Resist 26	Ruin 50	Secrete 42	Sign 25, 35	Spasm 42
Resolute 39	Rule 50	Section 31	Significant 27	Speak 31
Resonate 39	Ruminate 39	Secure 34, 46	Silence 24	Special 19
Respect 19	Run 50	Sedate 42	Silk 42	Specific 36
Respective 45	Ruthless 50	Seduce 31	Similar 30	Spectacle 31
Respire 39	Sacred 16	Seed 42	Simple 24	Speculate 36
Respond 29	Sad 35	Seem 42	Simulate 42	Speed 43
Responsible 29	Sadist 24	Seismic 31	Sincere 22	Spend 20
Restore 39	Safe 35	Select 24	Single 35	Spine 43
Restrict 19	Sage 31	Self 24	Sister 42	Spirit 24
Retain 50	Saint 35	Senate 42	Site 42	Splendid 36
Retaliate 50	Sale 35	Senior 42	Six 19	

Sponge 43	Submit 43	Symbol 36	Thresh 50	Tremor 39
Spontaneous 43	Subscribe 43	Symmetry 37	Thrift 50	Trench 44
Spy 44	Substance 36	Symptom 43	Thrill 50	Trend 51
Stable 18	Subtle 43	Synthetic 36	Throne 51	Tribe 51
Stagnate 43	Suburb 43	Synchronize 43	Thug 50	Trick 39
Standard 43	Subvert 43	System 31	Thunder 50	Triple 51
Star 43	Succeed 17	Table 39	Tight 18	Triumph 51
Start 43	Suck 43	Tactile 50	Tile 50	Trivial 39
State 43	Sudden 43	Talk 50	Timid 22	Troop 39
Statistic 31	Suffer 27	Tame 50	Tin 50	Troth 48
Statue 43	Suffice 31	Tangle 32	Tire 39	Trouble 51
Steady 31	Suggest 36	Tantalize 50	Titilate 50	Trust 15, 51
Steep 43	Suicide 36	Tax 39	Title 32, 50	Truth 29
Sterile 36	Suit 31	Technical 14	Tolerate 15, 23	Tube 51
Stern 43	Sulk 20	Teach 39	Tone 15	Type 37
Stick 43	Sullen 20	Tedious 50	Tonsil 50	Understand 29
Stiff 36	Sultan 43	Teens 50	Top 50	Union 50
Stigma 36	Summary 43	Telegram 33	Topic 50	Unite 23
Stimulus 36	Sumptuous 43	Telepathy 50	Torture 29	Use 20
Stock 43	Super 43	Telephone 39	Total 39	Vacant 17
Stoic 36	Superficial 43	Temper 19	Touch 39	Valiant 43
Stone 43	Superior 34	Tempt 39	Tough 50	Valid 22
Strain 43	Supervise 36	Ten 50	Tourism 50	Value 11
Strange 31	Supple 43	Tenable 39	Toxic 15	Vapour 20
Strangle 36	Supply 43	Tender 39	Traction 34	Vary 14
Strategy 31	Support 34	Tense 50	Trade 50	Vegan 25
Streak 43	Suppose 24	Term 10	Tradition 50	Vein 43
Stretch 43	Suppress 14	Terminal 39	Tragedy 50	Velvet 43
Strict 31	Supreme 36	Terror 19	Traitor 16	Vent 43
Strike 43	Sure 43	Test 50	Transcend 50	Verb 43, 47
String 43	Surf 43	Testate 50	Transfer 50	Verify 22
Strip 43	Surgical 36	Theatre 50	Transform 50	Victor 43
Strong 43	Surmount 43	Theology 18, 50	Transgress 50	View 39
Stub 36	Surreal 36	Theory 21	Transition 29	Vigil 25
Stubborn 43	Survive 36	Therapy 50	Translate 50	Vigour 35
Study 36	Suspect 36	Thermostat 50	Transmit 51	Villain 20
Stuff 43	Suspend 43	Thick 16	Transparent 39	Violate 25
Stump 36	Sweat 43	Thief 50	Transport 51	Virus 31
Stupor 24	Sweet 31	Thin 16	Trap 39	Visible 31
Style 24	Swell 43	Think 29	Trauma 51	Visual 17
Suave 43	Swift 43	Thorough 50	Travel 51	Vital 41
Subjective	Swim 43	Thrall 44	Treasure 51	Vitreous 44
Sublime 43	Sycophant 43	Three 23	Treat 49	Vivid 44

Voice 14
Volunteer 31
Vulgar 44
Vulnerable 35
Warm 44
Wary 44
Waste 31
Watch 44
Weak 25
Weary 31
Weave 44
Weed 44
Weigh 31
Well 44
West 20
Whale 44
Whine 44
Whistle 44
White 31
Who 44
Wicked 44
Wide 31
Wild 20
Will 20
Win 44
Wing 44
Wire 32
Wise 32
Wit 20
Witch 37
Woman 20
Wonder 32
Wood 31
Wool 44
Word 25
Work 32
Worse 44
Worth 20
Wrap 44
Wreck 44
Wrestle 32
Wretch 32
Write 25, 39

Wrong 19
Young 32
Youth 32

INDEX NOTE

I haven't included the real world section in the index as it is easy to look up the heading and trace down the columns for reference. However the diminishing size of the main section's columns, makes it more difficult to find specific, related words in the text, so that an index was needed for that as a matter of course.